THE
CHOSEN
FAST

21-DAY GUIDE ON PRAYER & FASTING

Raeni Bankole

THE
CHOSEN
FAST

21-DAY GUIDE ON PRAYER & FASTING

Raeni Bankole

Dewalette Creations

The Chosen Fast

Copyright © 2014 by Raeni Bankole
Paperback ISBN: 978-0-9886747-5-2
eBook ISBN: 978-0-9886747-6-9

Published by Dewalette Creations
Phone: 630-481-6305
Email: info@dewalette.com
www.dewalette.com

Cover Design by GodKulture Creative Agency

Printed in the United States of America

DEDICATION

This book is dedicated to the Holy Spirit my Teacher, the One who instructs my rein in the night seasons. You are my Helper, who knit my story together from my mother's womb and You have chosen to use every single detail for Your glory. I have personally seen You turn an empty jar of clay into a walking wonder because of Your indwelling presence.

I am eternally grateful for Your love.

ACKNOWLEDGMENTS

I am grateful for my loving husband and God-given friend Adebowale Bankole. I am truly blessed to be your wife and I can never truly express my gratitude for your unwavering love. I am indeed privileged to be walking this journey with such a great man of God who has allowed me to answer the call of destiny.

And to our children - you are truly a joy to hold and behold! You will become all that our Maker has called you to be. I am so glad that even from a young age you have become wise in His holy scriptures.

I truly appreciate the watchmen of the Nehemiah Troop Prayer Ministry who went through the daily discoveries of God's treasure with me; we will touch the world with the fire of His zeal.

I celebrate the destiny helpers that God bundled as the voice of encouragement in my life – my dear friend Foluke Aremu, covenant friends like Alison and Dina Ogbeifun, visionary leaders from Kingsword International Church, ThyBalm and ThyPreciousJewel. Thank you for believing in my dream.

I am indebted to the Winners' Chapel family for my foundation and the Redeemed Christian Church of God family for being my training ground.

I appreciate those who sowed unusual seeds into my life and ministry across the nations – Kemi Adeniji, Tomike Olagundoye, Founande Oladipupo and Remi Famoriyo. The Lord God will honor your seeds in Jesus' name. My selfless aunt Yomi Abraham, your seed will forever speak! As for my parents and siblings, you are a proof that prayer works!

I would like to acknowledge the team at Dewalette Creations for working tirelessly on this manuscript day and night to meet this out-of-the-world publication deadline. You were sent to me by Providence!

To all who have been a blessing to this child of destiny one way or another and I have failed to mention you by name - THANK YOU!

CONTENTS

FOREWORD

God declared in Genesis 1:3, "Let there be light." Those words were so powerful that they literally began to reshape and reform the entire planet that had been ruined by the devil, who was once an archangel known as Lucifer. Lucifer had so much influence in the pre-adamic world that a third of the angels followed him in rebellion against God. He was dissatisfied with his placement and authority, so he set out to exalt his throne to be like God. His attempt to overthrow God did not only fail but it left the earth in ruin.

Genesis 1:2a - *The earth was without form and void; and darkness was on the face of the deep.*

However, God refused to accept the state of ruin that the earth was left in because of the devil's rebellion. In contrary, He began to recreate the planet through the release of words filled with faith. At the foundation of these words were "Let there be light". Light, in this context, is not just physical. Rather, it is a spiritual force that constitutes the very nature of deity. 1 John 1:5 declares that God is light and in Him there is no darkness. Psalm 104:2 also states that God is wrapped with light as with a garment. God was releasing a spiritual force filled with His nature when He said, "Let there be light." He was literally releasing His nature over the planet to bring about the desired restoration.

Psalms 119:130a - *The entrance of your Word gives light;*

The light of God is the only solution to the darkness that the enemy of our soul brought over the planet. For this singular purpose, God has inspired Raeni to put Word capsules together that are capable of releasing light over your situation. The contents of this book will provide more than information for your situation. Beyond information, you will experience revelation that will cause a positive revolution in your life as you apply the principles in this book.

I can assure you that if you will be diligent with the instructions in this book, your heart will be flooded with the revelation of God's word. This will lead to an impartation of divine power into your life that supplies all that has to do with life in the order of God.

> **2 Peter 1:3,4a** - *As His divine power has given to us all things that pertain to life and godliness, through the knowledge of Him who called us by glory and virtue, ⁴by which have been given to us exceedingly great and precious promises, that through these you may be partakers of the divine nature.*

God has indeed chosen a fast so that your light can break forth everywhere. I believe that the command of light that God gave in the first chapter of Genesis is still on. So, receive that light as you attend to the precepts of 'The Chosen Fast'.

Dr. Kay Ijisesan
President, KingsWord Ministries International

INTRODUCTION

Is anyone among you suffering? Let him pray
- James 5:13

The Chosen Fast is the divine prescription for complete healing in every area of your life according to the Word of God.

Isaiah 58:6-8 - *"Is this not the fast that I have chosen: To loose the bonds of wickedness, To undo the heavy burdens, To let the oppressed go free, And that you break every yoke? Is it not to share your bread with the hungry, And that you bring to your house the poor who are cast out; When you see the naked, that you cover him, And not hide yourself from your own flesh? Then your light shall break forth like the morning, Your healing shall spring forth speedily, And your righteousness shall go before you; The glory of the Lord shall be your rear guard.*

As you follow the chapters laid out in this book, my prayer is that you discover the Healer's manual for the specific area of need in your life. I pray that the Holy Spirit will grant you insight to the required doses for your situation and a completely new you will emerge at the end of this fast. You can consider the prayer points in this book as the medicine you need to apply to that area of **disease**. Disease comes from two root words that connect to mean the opposite of ease (**dis-ease**). In order to have ease after seeing a medical doctor, you must apply the medicine in the order it was prescribed. For you to have ease in your life, family, marriage, career, destiny, finances, business, academics or ministry, you must follow the instruction slip that comes with your medication; in this case, it is the Word of God.

Jesus Christ is the Great Physician and Master Healer; He is also known as Jehovah Rapha or Jehovah Ropheka - the Lord that heals. The medicine is the Word of God and the Pharmacist dispensing the healing drug or medicine is the Holy Spirit. He takes all the credit for mixing the medicine in the right proportion for effective healing. You can look at this book as the instruction slip that accompanies your medication. The real cure for your ailment is the Word of God!

The Word of God is also described as water (Ephesians 5:26), milk (1 Peter 2:2), meat (Hebrews 5:12), honey (Psalm 119: 103) and sometimes fire (Jeremiah 23:29).

Water is refreshing.
Milk is for growth.
Meat is for strength.
Honey is for exploits.
Fire is for processing or purifying.

The purpose of this 21-day prayer and fasting manual is to help you discover God in a deeper way. The Creator's intent when He made man was to have a relationship with Him (Genesis 3:8). And that intent has not changed even after man fell into sin. The redemption plan was to mend the broken relationship between God and man. However, the extent to which you seek Him is the extent to which you will discover Him.

Proverbs 8:17 - *I love those who love me, And those who seek me diligently will find me.*

WHAT IS FASTING?

Fasting is abstaining from food and water for a season. The Chosen Fast is not to get your wish list granted or to bribe God for your needs to be met. Fasting does not change God's mind; fasting changes you! During a fast, you subdue your flesh but your spirit (the true you) comes alive. Fasting silences the voice of the flesh so that the voice of the Spirit is amplified. It intensifies our ability to perceive the manifest presence of God.

Fasting is primarily an act of willing abstinence or reduction from certain or all food and/or drink for a period of time. An absolute fast is normally defined as abstinence from all food and liquid for a defined period, ranging from a single day (24 hours) to several days. Other fasts may be partially restrictive, limited to particular foods or substances. The fast may also be intermittent in nature. Fasting practices may preclude sexual intercourse and other activities as well as food.

There are some things that will not yield or leave without fasting accompanied with prayer. Jesus, addressing His disciples when they could not heal a boy that was troubled by demonic spirits said, "However, this kind does not go out except by prayer and fasting" (Matthew 17:21). In order for you to address some satanic afflictions and destroy the works of the flesh, you must be willing to fast and pray. Abstaining from food without praying is tantamount to hunger strike; it is not productive. In fact, it is destructive and can impact your physical health negatively. There is an acceptable fast according to scriptures and by the time you are through with this book, you would have mastered the basic principles of fasting.

Fasting changes you, not God! Like the word *fast*, you become swift as the eagle; you become light as a feather but able to lift heavy weights.

WHAT IS PRAYER?

Prayer is a two-way communication between God and man. If it is one-way, it is not a dialogue but a monologue. PRAYER IS NOT "Gimme, gimme, my name is Jimmy!" Prayer is enforcing God's will on the earth.

Prayer is a dynamic sweet communion that empowers and liberates, not a chore or some religious obligation to fulfill. When I pray, I'm loving on my Father! When I pray, I'm addressing specific situations and taking over nations. When I pray, I'm crushing the devil. When I pray, I'm speaking God's Word to strengthen my heart. No wonder Jesus prayed all the time!

Prayer unlocks the double doors of supernatural provision and the secret riches of kings.

> **Isaiah 45:1-3** - *"Thus says the Lord to His anointed, To Cyrus, whose right hand I have held—To subdue nations before him and loose the armor of kings, To open before him the double doors, So that the gates will not be shut: 'I will go before you and make the crooked places straight; I will break in pieces the gates of bronze and cut the bars of iron. I will give you the treasures of darkness and hidden riches of secret places, that you may*

know that I, the Lord, Who call you by your name, Am the God of Israel.

From the secrets you get from this book, you will be satisfied with both physical and spiritual food for the rest of your life!

Psalm 78:23-25 *—Yet He had commanded the clouds above, and opened the doors of heaven, Had rained down manna on them to eat, and given them of the bread of heaven. Men ate angels' food; He sent them food to the full.*

By the knowledge discovered in this prayer manual, you will control kingdom wealth according to Isaiah 60:11,

Therefore your gates shall be open continually; They shall not be shut day or night, That men may bring to you the wealth of the Gentiles, And their kings in procession.

Man is made in God's image and likeness – man is spirit, has a soul and lives in a body. The Bible says God is spirit and they that worship him must worship Him in spirit and in truth. The Father is seeking spirits to worship Him – not mere mortals, not lip service and not churchgoers. He is not looking for people to just wear a club badge or carry a banner around for Him saying I am a Christian. He is looking for those who will represent Him, be like Him and manifest His true nature to the world. As a believer, you are God's offspring – His child, His Son – and the entire world is waiting for your manifestation. You must be unveiled to your world.

A caterpillar lives in a chrysalis, or what is commonly known as the cocoon, for a season and after a while, its true nature is unveiled as a butterfly, in true beauty and grace. So also after a season of separation in the Holy Ghost cocoon or chrysalis, you will come out fairer and stronger than your peers in Jesus' name. Your true nature and spiritual essence will manifest. You will fulfill your true calling in life and destiny as you go on this journey of discovery and the power to win in every area of life will be easily accessible to you from the Throne Room of the Master of the Universe.

Are you saved? Do you know the Great Eagle described in Deuteronomy 32:10? Is He your savior? He wants you to know Him intimately as the Giver behind the gifts. He desires that you abide in His presence more than craving His presents. Most people seek His hands but He wants to reveal to you the secrets of His heart. He died so that you can have life – supernatural abundant life here on earth and eternal life after your assignment here is done. He loves you and died for you. He wants to lead you and help you ride the storms. He wants to empower you and transform you. He wants to make a star out of you. Will you let Him? Will you give Him room? Without Him being your Lord and Savior, you will just be going through the rituals of this fast like any ancient religion; it would be a mere hunger strike.

If you are ready to let Him into your heart, please say this prayer out loud:

> *Lord Jesus, I accept you as my Lord and Savior. Deliver me and save me from my sins. Forgive me and wash me with your blood. Set me free from my past and grant me a new beginning in you. Reveal the new me now that I am born again to serve the living God in Jesus' name. Amen!*

Welcome to the family of God!

HOW TO YOU USE THIS BOOK

You may adopt different methods with this book:

1. Extended: 21 days fasting and prayer for permanent breakthrough to a new level.
2. Intermittent: Once a week fasting and prayer regimen; pick a topic of interest.
3. Devotional: Daily reading outline accompanied with optional fasting and prayer.
4. Bible Study Manual: For families or small groups on a journey of discovery, topic by topic.

DAY 1
PRAISE AND THANKSGIVING

Thanksgiving and praise attract divine attention! To engage the Man of War in a season of warfare, you must command His attention. Psalm 100:4 says we should *"Enter into His gates with thanksgiving, and into His courts with praise"*. In order to engage divine help, you must sound an alarm of praise. As you embark on this 21-day journey, you will be empowered to deal with all manner of outstanding issues and win any spiritual warfare. However, you must follow the precepts laid out according to Numbers 10:9,

> *When you go to war in your land against the enemy who oppresses you, then you shall sound an alarm with the trumpets, and you will be remembered before the Lord your God, and you will be saved from your enemies.*

We must enter into His gates with thanksgiving (Psalm 100:4).

PRAYER is the KEY that unlocks the door to the SUPERNATURAL! "Praise" is the plural of "pray". In other words, praise is a higher level of prayer. Prayer unlocks the doors but praise blasts open every obstruction in the path of the righteous and demolishes every yoke or bondage of the enemy as recorded in Acts 16:25-26,

But at midnight Paul and Silas were praying and singing hymns to God, and the prisoners were listening to them. [26] Suddenly there was a great earthquake, so that the foundations of the prison were shaken; and immediately all the doors were opened and everyone's chains were loosed.

PRAYER IS A BOMB BUT PRAISE IS DYNAMITE! Bomb destroys a smaller area while dynamite impacts larger areas. Praise is a weapon in spiritual warfare according to Psalm 149:6,

Let the high praises of God be in their mouth, and a two-edged sword in their hand;

Some doors may prove difficult to open with prayer but such cases cannot resist praise. Those doors need to be blown down in Praise Warfare!

Joshua 6:20 - *So the people shouted when the priests blew the trumpets. And it happened when the people heard the sound of the trumpet, and the people shouted with a great shout, that the wall fell down flat. Then the people went up into the city, every man straight before him, and they took the city.*

The combination code that the enemy cannot resist is praise from the mouth of the righteous.

Psalm 118:19-20 - *Open to me the gates of righteousness;I will go through them,And I will praise the Lord. This is the gate of the Lord,Through which the righteous shall enter.*

To gain access to the realm of the spirit, you must have the right keys or combination code. The trumpet of praise always compels divine attention.

Joel 2:1 - *Blow the trumpet in Zion, and sound an alarm in My holy mountain! Let all the inhabitants of the land tremble; For the day of the Lord is coming, For it is at hand.*

Several times when the children of God were faced with battles, they blew the trumpet and sounded an alarm. Praises bring your adversary cheaply to their knees. When you praise God, He will raise you! When the cops sound the siren on the earth, everyone steps aside. So also in the spirit realm, when you blow the siren of praise, problems bow, mountains flee and demons tremble.

2 Chronicles 20:22 - *Now when they began to sing and to praise, the Lord set ambushes against the people of Ammon, Moab, and Mount Seir, who had come against Judah; and they were defeated.*

Praises command divine presence. God chose Judah from the beginning to be his dwelling place (Psalm 114:2-8). Judah means praise and the Lion of the Tribe of Judah, the root of Jesse is here right now to inhabit our praise.

Psalm 22:3 - *But You are holy, O You Who dwell in the holy place where the praises of Israel are offered.*

You must make this an unusual praise, an uncommon praise - one that will catch the attention of the King of all kings and Lord of Lords! As you begin with this 21-day prayer and fasting manual, you must understand the importance of sounding the alarm of praise. On a daily basis, ensure that you don't barge into the presence with your list of demands but that you unlock the supernatural with the key of praise. Throughout these 21 days, make sure you engage His attention through praise! Give Him heartfelt praise from the depth of your being, engaging your spirit, soul and body! In your closet sing, chant, praise, dance, clap and prostrate before him like the 24 elders and the host of heaven! Say wonderful things to him, call him by His names. Declare His mighty works! Praise His holy name! Lift Jesus higher!

Here is an example of a praise chant:

My God and King!

He rides upon the wings of the mornings
The mountains and the hills skip as rams before him
When He whistles, we hear claps of thunder
He thunders in the clouds and the ignorant call him "Sango"
He quakes in the sea and the scientist call him "Tsunami"
When he is angry, the deep is shaken from within
The clouds are the dust of His feet (Nahum 1:3, NKJV)
My God and King!

Rock of ages
First and the last
Ageless one; the ancient of days that never grows bald nor wrinkles...
Beginning and the end;
The one who has been before the beginning began
Controller of the times and seasons
Master of the universe
Captain of the cosmos
Creator of heaven and earth
Possessor of heaven and earth

My God and King!
The General Superintendent of the whole galaxies
The heaven is His throne and the earth His footstool
The Governor among nations
The Prime Minister of all prime ministers
The King of all kings
The Lord of all lords
Sovereign
Majestic
My God and King!

DAY 1 PRAYER POINTS:

1. Thank You for keeping me to this day and giving me good health. I am grateful for the breath in me that money cannot buy. Thank You for the ransom paid for my life by the blood of Jesus.

2. Thank You, Lord, for the salvation of my soul and the ever-living blood of Jesus that is working in my life at all times, speaking mercy for me and vengeance for my enemies.

3. Thank You for provision, safety, protection, journey mercies and safe medical procedures whether major or minor – You gave me victory each time.

4. Thank You Jesus for eternal salvation and the grace to abide in You daily. Thank You for this chosen fast that will usher me to a new level and a deeper walk with You.

5. Thank You Jesus for being my great high priest, interceding for me daily before the throne and for deliverance from six and seven troubles!

Job 5:19 - *He shall deliver you in six troubles, Yes, in seven no evil shall touch you.*

6. I praise You for my family of orientation and procreation, I thank You for my family members – my spouse, children, parents and siblings.

7. Thank You, Lord, for uncommon friends and precious loved ones around me (Mention them). Thank You for my mentors and helpers of destiny.

8. Thank You for winning my impossible battles – known and unknown. Thank You Lord for fighting all the battles arrayed against me from generations past.

9. I choose to praise You for all that is working right now and the things that look impossible in the physical but are perfected in the spiritual.

10. I am grateful for experiencing the four seasons of this year and I give You praise for the crowning blessings that will unfold before this year runs out.

11. Thank You for the grace and empowerment made available to go through the 21 days of prayer and fasting in Jesus' name.

Give thanks for answered prayers!

DAY 2
THE PRAYER WATCHES

Today, we will be looking at something called The Prayer Watches. What does it mean to watch? To watch means to be alert and attentive. In Matthew 26:40-41, Jesus came to the disciples and found them sleeping, and He said to Peter, *"What! Could you not watch with Me one hour? Watch and pray, lest you enter into temptation. The spirit indeed is willing, but the flesh is weak."*

If you have embarked on these 21 days of fasting and prayer, you cannot afford to just go through it as a hunger strike. You must prayerfully watch with perseverance in order to receive God's will for your life, your family, your church, your nation and generation. Fasting without praying with efficacy is tantamount to hunger strike! There are eight (8) prayer watches in 24 hours at every three-hour interval:

- 12 a.m. – Midnight
- 3 a.m.
- 6 a.m.
- 9 a.m.
- 12 p.m. – Noon
- 3 p.m.
- 6 p.m.
- 9 p.m.

There are several scriptures that referred to the different prayer watches like the Psalmist mentioned the night watches (Psalm 119:148), the morning watches (Psalm 130:6). Proverbs 8:34 speaks of watching all day long,

> *Blessed is the man who listens to me, Watching daily at my gates, Waiting at the posts of my doors.*

When Jesus was speaking to the disciples just before He was crucified, He also alluded to the prayer watches in Matthew 26:38,

> *Then He said to them, "My soul is exceedingly sorrowful, even to death. Stay here and watch with Me."*

We are not expected to recline until testimonies abound and victories are won permanently in the physical according to Isaiah 62:6-7,

> *I have set watchmen on your walls, O Jerusalem; They shall never hold their peace day or night. You who make mention of the Lord, do not keep silent, and give Him no rest till He establishes and till He makes Jerusalem a praise in the earth.*

This means we must not only pray when we fast, but we must engage ourselves in praise warfare! Remember what praise achieved for Paul and Silas in the midnight watch in Acts 16:25. We must engage the help of the Holy Spirit during these 21 days in midnight praise and prayer warfare.

Also observe that Elijah observed this simple principle (1 Kings 18:36). Daniel also practiced it (Daniel 6:10) and he had uncommon prayer results and revelations that have transcended generations. In the New Testament, Jesus and the disciples practiced it as well.

Acts 3:1 - *Now Peter and John went up together to the temple at the hour of prayer, the ninth hour.*

1 Thessalonians 5:6 says,

Therefore let us not sleep, as others do, but let us watch and be sober.

Sleep here not only refers to physical sleep but spiritual lukewarmness. You cannot walk with God and love sleep. He will wake you up at different watches to pray.

1 Thessalonians 5:7 - *For those who sleep, sleep at night, and those who get drunk are drunk at night.*

If you are confused about your destiny, calling or a particular assignment, you can embark on a fasting and prayer watch like in Habakkuk 2:1-2,

I will stand my watch and set myself on the rampart, and watch to see what He will say to me, and what I will answer when I am corrected. Then the Lord answered me and said: 'Write the vision and make it plain on tablets, that he may run who reads it.

You may observe all prayer watches in 15-20 minutes segments, but please ensure you set aside some time for at least one hour prayer during this fast on a daily basis. You must pay particular attention to the midnight watch (12 a.m.) because it is a very sensitive and powerful hour. Look at your place of origin or birth and identify the midnight hour there (for example, 5 or 6 p.m. in the United States may be the midnight hour in some place in Africa – take advantage of that prayer hour.) If you are experiencing strange battles, make sure you pray at that exact hour (5 or 6 p.m.) depending on the time zone of the place of your origin and you should do the same for the midnight hour at your place of residence. Use both watches well. Please engage in a personal night vigil at least once a week. Some battles can only be dealt with effectively at night.

Matthew 13:25 - *But while men slept, his enemy came and sowed tares among the wheat and went his way.*

The deed must be undone in the night watches. Jesus practiced this regularly during His earthly ministry.

Mark 1:35 - *Now in the morning, having risen a long while before daylight, He went out and departed to a solitary place; and there He prayed.*

No wonder He commanded such attention!

Please make sure you are fasting and praying this season. I am convinced that you will emerge as a different breed at the end of this journey. Remember Matthew 17:21 says,

…this kind goes not out but by fasting and prayer.

Some battles won't give way to regular *bread and butter* prayers.

DAY 2 PRAYER POINTS:

1. Thank You for the second day of this 21-day journey of the chosen fast. Thank You Lord for life, family and loved ones.

2. Thank You for granting me access to Your throne of mercy by the blood of the Lamb and for writing my name in the Lamb's book of life.

3. Thank You for every revelation and insight given to me through Your Word that leads me into perpetual victory.

4. Thank You for deliverance through the knowledge of Your finished work on the cross of Calvary. My life can never remain the same forever!

5. Father, empower me during these 21 days of fasting and prayer. Help me to observe the prayer watches by Your grace.

6. Lord, envelope me with your power to engage in spiritual warfare in the night watches. Man of war, fight all my strange battles!

7. Empower my spirit man with might and teach my fingers to fight and my hands to war. Empower my prayer life and teach me to profit in the place of prayer.

> **Psalm 18:34** - *He teaches my hands to make war, So that my arms can bend a bow of bronze.*

8. Grant me the spirit of grace and supplication to persevere in prayer and fasting – interceding for my location, nation and generation.

Zechariah 12:10 - *"And I will pour on the house of David and on the inhabitants of Jerusalem the Spirit of grace and supplication.*

9. Father Lord, baptize me with Your fire and let my prayer shake my nation and generation like Paul and Silas. Grant me the anointing of Daniel; make me a watchman in the order of Ezekiel.

10. As I observe the prayer watches with fasting, let the bond of wickedness (familiar, generational and territorial darkness) be broken and let every yoke be destroyed in Jesus' name.

Isaiah 58:6 - *"Is this not the fast that I have chosen: To loose the bonds of wickedness, To undo the heavy burdens, To let the oppressed go free, And that you break every yoke?*

11. Lord, like Elijah cause my prayer altar to catch fire. Let souls be won to the kingdom and let lives be preserved from collective calamity in Jesus' name.

12. Ask, seek and knock! Ask the Lord what you desire. Mention the specific areas before Him. He has offered us a blank check like Solomon!

Matthew 7:7-8 - *"Ask, and it will be given to you; seek, and you will find; knock, and it will be opened to you. For everyone who asks receives, and he who seeks finds, and to him who knocks it will be opened."*

Give thanks for answered prayers!

DAY 3
THE ACCEPTABLE FAST

Welcome to the third day of The Chosen Fast! Today is very significant because the Word of God says in Hosea 6:2-3,

> *After two days He will revive us; On the third day He will raise us up, That we may live in His sight. Let us know, let us pursue the knowledge of the Lord. His going forth is established as the morning; He will come to us like the rain, like the latter and former rain to the earth.*

My prayer is that as you pursue the Lord and seek His face concerning specific issues in your life, you will find Him. He will reveal Himself in His full glory like Moses. God seekers are always God-getters! If you seek Him diligently through prayer and fasting coupled with the knowledge of His Word with all your heart, you will find Him.

Why do we fast? Many times we think that fasting touches God or changes His mind or that we can use it to bribe Him. No! Completely wrong! Fasting changes you, not God!

Ezra 8:21 - *Then I proclaimed a fast there at the river of Ahava, that we might humble ourselves before our God, to seek from Him the right way for us and our little ones and all our possessions.*

Fasting humbles you and silences the flesh so that the spirit man can be empowered. Fasting does not and cannot pay God for our sins; that was why Christ died! Christ is the complete propitiation for our sins. Since Christ died, God is no longer angry with man. He was completely appeased when His only son died. Have you experienced a situation whereby someone offended you and your loved one spoke words or showed acts of kindness that made you let go of your hurt, not because the wrongdoer did anything but because the person you love or hold in high esteem made the move for atonement. So also God was completely pacified by the death of His son for you and I.

Fasting cannot to pacify God; His son finished that task over two thousand years ago. Instead, fasting subdues the flesh so that one's spirit can rule or come alive. Have you noticed that you are struggling with impatience, a stony heart, anger, lust or unforgiveness even as a believer? Then it is time to mortify the flesh through fasting and prayer. Or are you finding it hard to pray or study the Word? Then it is time to kill the flesh. I'm not talking about hunger strike here because you will only get crankier without food and miss the whole purpose of fasting. I'm talking about the chosen fast or what is called the acceptable fast according to Isaiah 58:1-14.

Fasting allows you to be renewed in strength like an eagle. Like the eagle, it is time to hibernate in order to rejuvenate. You must cautiously withdraw from the hullaballoo of mass media, social media, inner turmoil and outward noise to hear from the Teacher, our Instructor and Mentor.

Let us see from scriptures what this acceptable fast that produces true change entails:

Isaiah 58:1-14 - *Cry aloud, spare not; Lift up your voice like a trumpet; Tell My people their transgression, And the house of Jacob their sins. Yet they seek Me daily, And delight to know My ways, As a nation that did righteousness, And did not forsake the ordinance of their God. They ask of Me the ordinances of justice; They take delight in approaching God. 'Why have we fasted,' they say, 'and You have not seen? Why have we afflicted our souls, and You take no notice?' 'In fact, in the day of your fast you find pleasure, And exploit all your laborers. Indeed you fast for strife and debate, And to strike with the fist of wickedness. You will not fast as you do this day, To make your voice heard on high. Is it a fast that I have chosen, A day for a man to afflict his soul? Is it to bow down his head like a bulrush, And to spread out sackcloth and ashes? Would you call this a fast, And an acceptable day to the Lord? 'Is this not the fast that I have chosen: To loose the bonds of wickedness, To undo the heavy burdens, To let the oppressed go free, And that you break every yoke? Is it not to share your bread with the hungry, And that you bring to your house the poor who are cast out; When you see the naked, that you cover him, And not hide yourself from your own flesh? Then your light shall break forth like the morning, Your healing shall spring forth speedily, And your righteousness shall go before you; The glory of the Lord shall be your rear guard. Then you shall call, and the Lord will answer; You shall cry, and He will say, 'Here I am.' 'If you take away the yoke from your midst, The pointing of the finger, and speaking wickedness, If you extend your soul to the hungry And satisfy the afflicted soul, Then your light shall dawn in the darkness, And your darkness shall be as the noonday. The Lord will guide you continually, And satisfy your soul in drought, And strengthen your bones; You shall be like a watered garden, And like a spring of water, whose waters do not fail. Those from among you Shall build the old waste places; You shall raise up the foundations of many generations; And you shall be called* *the Repairer of the Breach, The Restorer of Streets to Dwell In. "If you turn away your foot from the Sabbath, From doing your pleasure on My holy day, And call the Sabbath a delight, The holy day of the Lord honorable, And shall honor Him, not doing your own ways, Nor finding your own pleasure, Nor speaking your own words, Then you shall delight yourself in the Lord; And I will cause you to ride on the high hills of the earth, And feed you with the heritage of Jacob your father. The mouth of the Lord has spoken."*

When you follow the proper principles outlined here, you will see the following effects: You become a power carrier and have changed character or leveled temperament, compassionate heart, good health, promotion, restoration, fulfillment of purpose in destiny, abundant supply, fruitfulness, renewed strength, ability to destroy yokes, power to pray for long hours, the grace to easily defeat sicknesses and diseases and cheaply cast out demons.

The vision of everything I'm doing in ministry today was delivered to me by the Holy Spirit through this scripture in a season of fasting and prayer in my second year in college, almost 20 years ago. This 21-day journey will be full of do-it-yourself pointers that if you follow correctly, you will not need to go and consult with man ever again about the matters of your life. If at all you will consult men, they will only be confirming what you have already heard from God in your own secret place. However, in order to operate with expertise the power and authority freely given us to us by Christ Jesus in Luke 10:19, we must engage the help of the Holy Spirit indwelling our spirit man. For His voice to become stronger and louder than the flesh, we must subdue the flesh through fasting. Knowing Him intimately will allow us to walk daily in the realm of exploits like Peter and Paul healing the sick with their shadows or clothing items.

It is time for us to move from the realm of common occurrences to the realm of supernatural exploits where men revere our God and demons fear us! Receive empowerment today! Never again will we go into fasting as a religious tradition of men but from today we will approach fasting as an empowering exercise profitable unto all things.

DAY 3 PRAYER POINTS:

1. Thank You, Lord, for the gift of salvation that enlisted me in the school of the spirit for supernatural exploits.

2. Thank You, Lord, for picking me up from the miry clay and setting my feet on the solid rock, putting a new song in my mouth over my family, marriage, business, career academics and ministry.

3. Thank You for hiding me under the shadow of Your wings and keeping me in the secret place of Your pavilion, far way from calamity, sicknesses and diseases.

4. Thank You for Your instructions that are making me wiser in the knowledge of the holy. Thank You for showing me the true purpose of fasting and prayer.

5. Father Lord, reveal the details of my life with precision during the course of this fasting and prayer. Grant me the precept upon precept, line upon line information that only you can give.

6. As I fast and pray, renew my strength like the eagle and cause me to be a high flyer in everything I do. Let me move from the realm of struggling to sweatlessly riding over storms, mountains and challenges that defeat others.

7. I operate with the strength that comes from the Holy Spirit in the inner man to fast and pray observing the prayer watches without distraction. I will not faint nor grow weary in my journey of discovery in You.

8. From today, I am transformed from one level of glory to another into the image of our Lord Jesus Christ, manifesting his will, character and glory. I increase in spiritual stature and wisdom, having favor with God and man.

9. As I engage in fasting and strategic prayer, all my stubborn enemies will be permanently defeated without remedy. Every evil arm is broken and withers away; every evil tongue is disgraced and condemned in Jesus' name.

10. I proclaim by the Spirit of the Lord that every evil altar erected to hurt me or my household receives the judgment fire of God and is shattered to pieces never to rise up again like the wall of Jericho in Jesus' name.

11. As I continue these 21 days of fasting and prayer, let the changes taking place within me become apparent to everyone around me. Let me become an effective ambassador of your glorious kingdom, attracting many to salvation.

12. *Speak to the Lord about all your areas of weakness (mention them before Him).* His grace is more than enough. Ask that your joy may be full!

Give thanks for answered prayers!

DAY 4
THE ALTAR OF THE LORD

Today is the fourth day of The Chosen Fast and we will be looking closely at The Altar of the Lord. My prayer is that you will not be tired or weary in this journey of discovery. All your heart's desires will be met and the God of Jacob will fulfill all your petitions in Jesus' name.

In Genesis 28, Jacob had an encounter with the Lord God of Heaven and earth at a place called Bethel and he built an altar there. Abraham built an altar everywhere He encountered God (Genesis 22:9); Isaac did the same (Genesis 26:24-25); Gideon did the same!

The interesting thing about the Lord's altar is that God shows up there...always! See Judges 6:22, 24,

> *Now Gideon perceived that He was the Angel of the Lord. So Gideon said, "Alas, O Lord God! For I have seen the Angel of the Lord face to face." So Gideon built an altar there to the Lord, and called it The-Lord-Is-Peace. To this day it is still in Ophrah of the Abiezrites.*

Do you have a personal altar? Or a family altar? If you don't have one, please start one today. It is your prayer altar of worship and meeting with the Lord!

It may be physical or symbolic. Build one now!

Now I need you to pay close attention to what happened afterward in Judges 6:25-28:

> *Now it came to pass the same night that the Lord said to him, "Take your father's young bull, the second bull of seven years old, and tear down the altar of Baal that your father has, and cut down the wooden image that is beside it; and build an altar to the Lord your God on top of this rock in the proper arrangement, and take the second bull and offer a burnt sacrifice with the wood of the image which you shall cut down." So Gideon took ten men from among his servants and did as the Lord had said to him. But because he feared his father's household and the men of the city too much to do it by day, he did it by night. And when the men of the city arose early in the morning, there was the altar of Baal, torn down; and the wooden image that was beside it was cut down, and the second bull was being offered on the altar which had been built.*

The strange battle troubling Gideon was due to household wickedness from his father's house. Jesus, speaking in Matthew 10:36, said that a man's enemies will be those of his own household. There is nothing more profound than that! When Gideon built an altar unto the Lord and destroyed the evil altar of his father's house, he began to win previously impossible battles. That strange battle you are facing will bow at the presence of the Lord today as you erect an altar unto the Lord of Host in your heart and in your home. I declare that every evil altar erected anywhere in the physical or spiritual realm against you and your household will come crumbling down today! I decree that such altars that hold your image, name or effigy will catch fire and burn to ashes in Jesus' name.

Let us take a quick look at another altar:

1 Samuel 5:2-5 - *When the Philistines took the ark of God, they brought it into the house of Dagon and set it by Dagon. And when the people of Ashdod arose early in the morning, there was Dagon, fallen on its face to the earth before the ark of the Lord. So they took Dagon and set it in its place again. And when they arose early the next morning, there was Dagon, fallen on its face to the ground before the ark of the Lord. The head of Dagon and both the palms of its hands were broken off on the threshold; only Dagon's torso was left of it. Therefore neither the priests of Dagon nor any who come into Dagon's house tread on the threshold of Dagon in Ashdod to this day.*

There are altars and there are altars! The highest altar is that of the Most High. That evil personality that took your name, picture or image before an evil altar will never recover from the outburst of God's rage. That altar is shattered by fire never to be rebuilt again. Like the wall of Jericho and the king who tried to rebuild it, they will start the foundation with their first and complete it with their last-born. I decree that every enemy of your destiny in Christ Jesus is in deep trouble because the Defender of the defenseless had stepped into your case!

Did you know that you could submit an evil report on the altar of the Lord? Like Hezekiah who was threatened by a monstrous king called Sennacherib in 2 Kings 19:14-15. After he prayed, that king died like a rat. What is that threat against you or that force that has stripped you bare of your possession, honor and dignity? They will be buried alive today at the altar of the Lord. Bring that medical report or that test result before the altar of the Lord; you will not be disappointed.

In 1 Kings 18:36, 38-39, when Elijah rebuilt the altar of the Lord and prayed, fire fell!

And it came to pass, at the time of the offering of the evening sacrifice, (the prayer watch) that Elijah the prophet came near and said, "Lord God of Abraham, Isaac, and Israel, let it be known this day that You are God in Israel and I am Your servant, and that I have done all these things at Your word. Then the fire of the Lord fell and consumed the burnt sacrifice, and the wood and the stones and the dust, and it licked up the water that was in the trench. Now when all the people saw it, they fell on their faces; and they said, "The Lord, He is God! The Lord, He is God!"

The fire swallowed up everything – water, bull, wood and all. If you offer your life in service to Him as a living sacrifice, you will carry His fire. If you offer your praise on the altar, God will smell a sweet aroma. If you offer your time, talent and treasures, He will bless the works of your hands and multiply you beyond your imagination. Remember Solomon in 1 Kings 3:3. He offered a 1000 burnt offerings and the Lord offered him a blank check. The altar of deliverance was built in every home while under the bondage of slavery in Egypt, after offering the Passover Lamb on the altar of the Lord. What happened? An explosion that took decades for Pharaoh and his army to recover from.

Today, Christ is our ultimate Passover Lamb and the Lord will always find pleasure on your altar because of Him. By His blood, let us go up and destroy all the high places that have demanded for our bloodline from generations past. As we mount up with wings as eagles with the sword of the spirit and the fire of the Holy Ghost, let us tear down all the evil altars of sickness, shame, pain, reproach, stagnation, limitation, bondage and evil trends. As you build the altar of the Lord in your home, laying the wood in order and pouring the water of His Word, He will answer you by fire.

DAY 4 PRAYER POINTS:

1. Thank You Jesus, for dying on the cross to redeem me from the power of darkness and translating me into the Kingdom of Your marvelous light.

2. Thank You Father, for going ahead of me to fight my battles and for being my rear-guard in all visible and invisible warfare.

3. Thank You Holy Spirit, for inner peace and the strength in my inner man to go on with the 21 days of fasting and observing the prayer watches.

4. Thank You for the blood of sprinkling that washes me clean from every collective covenant and household wickedness that runs in families.

5. Father Lord, I present myself as a living sacrifice on your altar today, laying down all the time, talent and treasure you have given to me in absolute surrender and worship.

6. Holy Spirit, ignite my prayer altar with Your fire and let my life be a constant display of the supernatural in words, thoughts and deeds. Let my life be a Jesus magnet, according to Acts 10:38.

7. Father Lord, I dedicate with fresh oil my family's prayer altar to you. As a royal priesthood and a holy nation unto our God,

I pray that the fire will never fizzle out but will intensify from today, like the altar of the Levites.

8. Heavenly Father, I submit every negative report at your altar today like Hezekiah; the medical reports from the doctors, the account reports from the bankers, the academic reports from my teachers, the legal reports from the lawyers, the eviction notice from the landlords, the appraisal and career reports from my employers. I choose to believe your report in Jesus' name.

9. Lord of Hosts who dwells between the Cherubim! Harass my harassers, contend with my contenders, frustrate my frustrations and shatter every evil altar troubling me from my father's house, mother's house and in-laws' house.

10. My Lord and my God, as I prostrate before Your altar of sacrifice and praise You, destroy all the forces of limitation, oppression and affliction against me. Silence every threat against me and swallow up every evil altar erected on my behalf.

11. I declare that every evil altar erected anywhere in the physical or spiritual realm against my household and me will come crumbling down today! I decree that such altars that hold my image, name or effigy will catch fire and burn to ashes in Jesus' name (*pray for spouse, children, siblings and parents as well*).

12. From today, no more divination or enchantment has any effect in my life in Jesus' name. By the blood of Jesus, I free myself, my husband and children from every captivity that has resulted from evil dedications at birth or through marriage.

Give thanks for answered prayers!

DAY 5
THIS CUP OF BLESSING

Today is the fifth day of The Chosen Fast. The number five is the number of grace and my prayer is that grace will be imparted to you as you seek Him diligently during this period. You may have questions about the proper way to approach this fast. It is simply abstaining from food till you have prayed effectively and studied the Word of God for the area of emphasis or challenge. You can take advantage of anointed teachings on the topic of interest with your Bible and notepad.

Regardless of the time you choose to break the fast, please ensure that you pray and study the Word as you fast, otherwise it will just be a religious ritual that will yield no tangible result. However, if you follow the steps outlined in the scriptures for the acceptable fast, you will have tremendous results. I encourage you to observe the prayer watches as much as your schedule permits you. You may also drink water when going through an extended fast. It is advisable not to go beyond three days without water – your body needs to remain hydrated to maintain proper functioning.

The topic for today is The Communion Table. It is referred to in scriptures as this cup of blessing.

1 Corinthians 10:16 - *The cup of blessing which we bless, is* *it not the communion of the blood of Christ? The bread which we break, is it not the communion of the body of Christ?*

You may be wondering, "What does The Communion have to do with my fasting and prayer? What role has The Communion got to play in winning all the dark battles arrayed against me?" In this chapter, we will attempt to address with efficacy the power in the cup of blessing. Let us start by taking a look at a type of the communion table displayed in Exodus 12:

Exodus 12:5-8,11-14,35-36 - *Your lamb shall be without blemish, a male of the first year. You may take it from the sheep or from the goats. Now you shall keep it until the fourteenth day of the same month. Then the whole assembly of the congregation of Israel shall kill it at twilight. And they shall take some of the blood and put it on the two doorposts and on the lintel of the houses where they eat it. Then they shall eat the flesh on that night; roasted in fire, with unleavened bread and with bitter herbs they shall eat it. And thus you shall eat it: with a belt on your waist, your sandals on your feet, and your staff in your hand. So you shall eat it in haste. It is the Lord's Passover. For I will pass through the land of Egypt on that night, and will strike all the firstborn in the land of Egypt, both man and beast; and against all the gods of Egypt I will execute judgment: I am the Lord. Now the blood shall be a sign for you on the houses where you are. And when I see the blood, I will pass over you; and the plague shall not be on you to destroy you when I strike the land of Egypt. 'So this day shall be to you a memorial; and you shall keep it as a feast to the Lord throughout your generations. You shall keep it as a feast by an everlasting ordinance. Now the children of Israel had done according to the word of Moses, and they had asked from the Egyptians articles of silver, articles of gold, and clothing. And the Lord had given the people favor in the sight*

of the Egyptians, so that they granted them what they requested.
Thus they plundered the Egyptians.

Look at what happened! Previously, Moses had been fighting the forces and demons of Egypt with different plagues but they were able to bounce back after those plagues. But after the Lord's Passover, Pharaoh bowed out in defeat. First of all, the firstborn died in every single Egyptian household. I declare that if your evil pursuers don't repent from following you, their life will be given in exchange for yours in the name of Jesus! Then wherever the blood was seen, the angel of death passed over. You bear the marks of our Lord Jesus Christ in your body so death cannot touch you and evil will not slay any member of your family. Rather, the angels of death will fight strange battles for you and defeat every forces of darkness in your life because of the Lord of Hosts.

Next, the children of Israel were released suddenly from the bondage of the taskmaster, from hard labor and slavery. I declare that anyone experiencing any form of bondage – physical, spiritual, emotional or psychological – is set free in Jesus' mighty name. That job situation that you are going through or the marital affliction that keeps repeating itself like an evil trend in your family line is broken today by the blood of Jesus! Notice in the verse of scripture above that the wealth of the oppressor was transferred to the children of Israel sweatlessly. That wealth was to be used to build God's tabernacle as the Israelites journeyed to The Promised Land, not to build the golden calf. If God entrusts you with His wealth, it is to promote His kingdom and not for it to become your idol. They were also fed with manna continuously. They enjoyed divine protection by angels and divine guidance with the pillar of fire and cloud. None was feeble among them and God rebuked kings for their sake. The Lord's Passover is so empowering! Jesus is our Passover Lamb and He died for us on the cross of Calvary. Before He died, He gave this same ordinance to His disciples as revealed to Paul in 1 Corinthians 11:23-26:

> For I received from the Lord that which I also delivered to you: that the Lord Jesus on the same night in which He was betrayed took bread; and when He had given thanks, He broke it and said, "Take, eat; this is My body which is broken for you; do this in remembrance of Me." In the same manner He also took the cup after supper, saying, "This cup is the new covenant in My blood. This do, as often as you drink it, in remembrance of Me." For as often as you eat this bread and drink this cup, you proclaim the Lord's death till He comes.

It is very crucial for the believer to partake of The Communion on a regular basis and not once a month or ceremonially, as we have been made to believe. The apostles broke bread daily, from house to house (Acts 2:46). Jesus, addressing His disciples in John 6:53-58, said,

> ...Most assuredly, I say to you, unless you eat the flesh of the Son of Man and drink His blood, you have no life in you. Whoever eats My flesh and drinks My blood has eternal life, and I will raise him up at the last day. For My flesh is food indeed, and My blood is drink indeed. He who eats My flesh and drinks My blood abides in Me, and I in him. As the living Father sent Me, and I live because of the Father, so he who feeds on Me will live because of Me. This is the bread which came down from heaven—not as your fathers ate the manna, and are dead. He who eats this bread will live forever.

The cup of blessing imparts eternal life and longevity. It is like an intravenous injection (I.V) that resuscitates the believer from within. It infuses wisdom and power to the consumer. The Bible clearly states that Jesus is the wisdom and the power of God.

> **1 Corinthians 1:24,30** - *But to those who are called, both Jews and Greeks, Christ the power of God and the wisdom of God. But of Him you are in Christ Jesus, who became for us wisdom from God—and righteousness and sanctification and redemption.*

So when you eat His flesh and drink His blood, you become more like Him; you manifest His divine nature. If you are a student, you can tap into His wealth of wisdom and supernatural intelligence. Remember that when He broke bread with the disciples, their eyes became open (Luke 24:30-31). It wasn't their physical eyes that were opened, but the eyes of their mind.

When we eat the bread with understanding, it has the ability to release divine provision and disarm our enemies without sweat. Jesus said, "*...as often as you do it you proclaim the Lord's death until He comes.*" What does the death of Christ represent? Vengeance on our enemies! He spoiled principalities and powers triumphing over them in victory! He broke every yoke of sicknesses and diseases! He brought us out of darkness into His marvelous light!

He redeemed us from the curse of the law! He wore the crown of thorns on his head or brain so that our brains can perform with super speed, even better than Adam's. He became poor for us to become rich. He died young so that we can live long. He shed his blood on the ground that was cursed so that we don't have to operate under the curse of sweating and toiling anymore. He died without offspring or a wife so you can enjoy marital bliss. He has the church as His bride and we are His offspring through salvation. He paid the price in full so we don't have to bear the shame and guilt of sin anymore. We are completely free! Free to live in dominion and fulfill His assignment for our lives and the church as a whole.

This cup of blessing also imparts enabling grace and uncommon strength to go on long fasts and pray through the watches, just like Jesus did. The first time I ever went on a personal forty-day fast, I became faint by day ten (10) but the Lord instructed me to start taking the Communion daily and I was supernaturally strengthened to finish strong! You can do it as well. You just need a simple fruit of the vine juice (non-alcoholic) to represent the blood and simple bread or cracker to represent the flesh.

From today, every time you fast, make sure you break the fast with the Holy Communion and you will see the difference. The Communion Table is an ordinance the Bible says to teach to your children and observe it in your generations. As often as you do so, you are enforcing your victory in Christ Jesus. Don't get into the religion of it like Apostle Paul said – eating it carelessly. Instead, do it with reverence and understanding according to scriptures. My prayer is that your health will spring forth speedily as you observe this chosen fast. You will be like a watered garden whose waters fail not and blossom like willows by the watercourses!

DAY 5 PRAYER POINTS:

1. Thank You Lord, for dying for me on the cross of Calvary, disgracing and disarming principalities and powers, triumphing over them in it on my behalf (Colossians 2:15).

2. Thank You for the cup of blessing and the bread that infuses supernatural abilities to my spirit, soul and body! Thank You for quickening me from mortality to immortality!

3. Thank You Father, for hiding your mystery in the simple things that you have ordained to defeat the enemy of our faith. Thank You for the flesh and blood of Jesus!

4. Thank You for the Blood of Sprinkling that speaks better things than the blood of Abel, speaking mercy for me and vengeance for my enemies. I plead the blood of Jesus over myself, my husband and children! I plead the blood of the Passover Lamb over everything that concerns me.

5. I declare that I enjoy the favor promised in Exodus 3:21. I will not go empty from this table in Jesus' name. Emptiness and lack become plenty and abundance. I'm not only a carrier of blessing, but a channel of blessing to my generation.

> **Exodus 3:21** - *And I will give this people favor in the sight of the Egyptians; and it shall be, when you go, that you shall not go empty-handed.*

6. I receive wisdom, knowledge and understanding from the communion table. From today, I have eye-opening experiences and manifest an excellent spirit in Jesus' name. I have quick understanding.

7. As I pursue the Lord in this fast, strength is multiplied for me. The inspiration of the Almighty flows within me like a living spring flushing out every slothfulness, lukewarmness and sickness in Jesus' name. My health springs forth speedily!

8. Let the blood of Jesus be my I.V (intravenous injection) and the flesh of Jesus be all the medicine I will ever need for divine healing. As I swallow this divine pill, let every seed of sickness dry up to their roots in Jesus' name.

9. Let me feast at Your table daily and enjoy the power and grace that comes from eating the flesh and blood of Jesus that is more powerful than Manna. My children will never know lack and my generation will never beg for bread.

10. Father Lord, let Your pillar of fire go ahead of me and Your pillar of cloud cover me as I take giant steps of faith in my journey from here. Order my steps into greatness and establish my feet in high places.

11. Lord of hosts, take over my dark battles and visit the assembly of the wicked with the vengeance of the Passover. If they will not repent, visit them with Your angels; give them an unforgettable visit like You visited Pharaoh!

12. From this table, I contact uncommon favor that produces the power to get wealth and my household becomes a lighthouse in the darkness of this world. Many will come to the saving knowledge of Christ through our testimonies (Acts 2:46-47).

Give thanks to God for answered prayers!

DAY 6
SHADOW OF THE ALMIGHTY

Today is the sixth day of The Chosen Fast. Six is the number of man because God created man in His image and after His likeness on the sixth day. My prayer is that you will fulfill the purpose for which He created you. You will manifest the glory of the Lord, the true essence of His majesty. You will fulfill your divine destiny as an individual and your generation will celebrate the unique impact that God made you for. You were born in due season and the best time to live your life as He ordained it is now! God saw a problem before the foundation of the world and He conceived a solution and that solution package is you. Go and manifest to your world in Jesus' name!

In this chapter, we will be looking closely at the concept of the Shadow of the Almighty. What is a shadow? It is a dark figure or image cast on the ground or surface by a body intercepting light. It can also represent a period of gloom or doubt like in the saying "Without a *shadow* of doubt". Doubt normally cast a shadow on one's mind.

Shadow can also mean shelter, protection or sanctuary like finding shade from the heat of the sun under a tree. It can also mean to follow someone secretly in order to watch over that person.

What is the Shadow of the Almighty? The Bible describes His humongous and mega-super size in Isaiah 66:1,

> *Thus says the Lord: "Heaven is My throne, And earth is My footstool. Where is the house that you will build Me? And where is the place of My rest?*

Can you take a minute to imagine how great He is? He is great; the Master of the universe; Emperor on wings. What can touch you or who can find you under the shadow that He casts?

The main text for our meditation is Psalm 91:1-16,

> *He who dwells in the secret place of the Most High Shall abide under the shadow of the Almighty. I will say of the Lord, "He is my refuge and my fortress; My God, in Him I will trust." Surely He shall deliver you from the snare of the fowler And from the perilous pestilence. He shall cover you with His feathers, And under His wings you shall take refuge; His truth shall be your shield and buckler. You shall not be afraid of the terror by night, Nor of the arrow that flies by day, Nor of the pestilence that walks in darkness, Nor of the destruction that lays waste at noonday. A thousand may fall at your side, And ten thousand at your right hand; But it shall not come near you. Only with your eyes shall you look, And see the reward of the wicked. Because you have made the Lord, who is my refuge, Even the Most High, your dwelling place, No evil shall befall you, Nor shall any plague come near your dwelling; For He shall give His angels charge over you, To keep you in all your ways. In their hands they shall bear you up, Lest you dash your foot against a stone. You shall tread upon the lion and the cobra, The young lion and the serpent you shall trample*

underfoot. "Because he has set his love upon Me, therefore I will deliver him; I will set him on high, because he has known My name. He shall call upon Me, and I will answer him; I will be with him in trouble; I will deliver him and honor him. With long life I will satisfy him, And show him My salvation."

If there is any scripture you should memorize in the entire Bible, Psalm 91 is definitely one that I will recommend. You will be surprised how it shows up in the day of adversity and strengthens your heart. From it, we see that he who dwells in the secret place of the most high shall abide under the shadow of the Almighty. Where is the secret place? The place of worship, prayer, studying and meditating on the Word of God. This psalm is not a religious chant that you just throw around like a talisman. It is a double-edged sword that is in your mouth that you use in spiritual warfare.

The secret place is your altar unto the Lord. You must have that depth of intimacy with Him to enjoy the deep covering described in this chapter. The shadow of the Almighty is a place of quietness and, sometimes, absolute silence – like a protective parent will hush a child so that a wicked invader will not be able to trace them in the time of trouble. It may be characterized by occasional whispers of the still small voice.

There was a time in my life when I experienced extreme adversity and I thought the Lord had forsaken or forgotten me but He was actually hiding me in the shadow of His wings, in the secret place of His pavilion. The shadow is a dark place but it is not evil. It may look to the ordinary eye like the darkness of the evil one but it is not. The Bible distinguishes between the two types of darkness, the shadow of His wings is a place of quiet rest but that of the wicked is filled with cruelty, according to Psalm 74:20,

Have respect to the covenant; For the dark places of the earth are full of the haunts of cruelty.

Sometimes God withdraws Himself or makes Himself invisible or unheard because He wants us to grow our trust in Him.

2 Chronicles 32:31 - *However, regarding the ambassadors of the princes of Babylon, whom they sent to him to inquire about the wonder that was done in the land, God withdrew from him, in order to test him, that He might know all that was in his heart.*

The shadow of His wings is a place of divine protection and constant health. Under the shadow of the Almighty, we enjoy angelic intervention on a daily basis. It is a place where we are exempted from mass destruction and calamity. It is a place where we enjoy divine healing, divine health and especially, divine life! It is a place where the common flu or terminal sicknesses that destroy people out there cannot touch us.

It is a place where, despite engine failures on vehicles and planes, His angels bear us up on wings. It is place where we enjoy longevity. I have heard people say that God did not promise us long life - that is a lie of the enemy and nothing could be further from the truth! The Bible contains thousands of promises for us. Some say 4000 and others say 6000 and the truth may be somewhere in between those, but I dare to say that long life is one of them! Are there godly people who die young? Yes, but we will find out why when we see Him face-to-face.

Bible scholars believe that Psalm 91 was written by Moses (the author is unknown so they ascribed it to the writer of Psalm 90).

> **Psalm 90:7, 10** - *For we have been consumed by Your anger, And by Your wrath we are terrified. The days of our lives are seventy years; And if by reason of strength they are eighty years, Yet their boast is only labor and sorrow; For it is soon cut off, and we fly away.*

Here, Moses was explaining why the children of Israel were dying in the wilderness at 70-80 years old but he himself lived to be 120 years old.

God promised Abraham that he will live to a ripe full age and we are Abraham's seed through Christ Jesus, so we have a promise of a ripe full age. Many patriarchs lived long – Abraham lived to be 175; Isaac lived to be 180 years old and Jacob lived to be 147 years old. He is the God of Abraham, Isaac and Jacob and He is the same yesterday today and forever more. He allowed Job to see his children to the third and fourth generation.

Even when He was angry at the depravity of man in Genesis 6:3, He still had mercy and that was before the Jesus' atoning death for humanity. He wants you to live long to your satisfaction and in good health without terror or fear. God's desire is for us to be preserved for Him in order to affect and impact our world before Jesus returns to take us all home. Man was created to be exactly like God, to live forever in a state of heaven on earth but when sin came, God moved on to the next plan – nothing catches him off guard.

Ecclesiastes 3:11 - *He has made everything beautiful in its time. Also He has put eternity in their hearts, except that no one can find out the work that God does from beginning to end.*

In the shadow of the Almighty, we are guaranteed the power to tread upon serpents and scorpions. We can cheaply defeat the forces of darkness and cast out demons. He gave us power over the lion and every evil machination out there. In the shadow of the Most High, we are far from sleep disturbances. All the nightmares and night terrors are driven far away from our household. His Word keeps us strengthened and His great hands deflect every evil arrow. He covers us with His feathers.

A shadow is also known as an inseparable companion. It is a place of uncommon intimacy and knowledge of His secrets where you know things before they happen. It is a place of deliverance from strong battles. It is also a place of honor and divine lifting. It is a place of continuous answered prayers.

What sweet fellowship! What sweet communion and love! Such great promises! My prayer is that in these 21 days of fasting, you will discover that secret place – that depth of love and assurance that can only come from leaving the peripheral and entering into His most secret pavilion.

DAY 6 PRAYER POINTS:

1. Thank You heavenly Father for saving me from the darkness of this world and translating me into the kingdom of Your marvelous light!

2. Thank You for keeping me from all the dangers and perilous pestilence out there. Thank You for divine health, divine healing and divine life.

3. Thank You for watching over me and my entire household and for being our fortress in the day of trouble.

4. Thank You for the gift of salvation that allows me to draw near without any guilt into Your secret place of intimacy and love.

5. Father Lord, draw me nearer to the secret place of love and instruction – the place where you warn and reveal things before they happen.

6. Father Lord, keep all the days of my earthly journey hidden under the shadow of your wings and help me understand that You will never leave me nor forsake me.

7. I declare from today that I am excluded from every sickness and disease that spreads easily out there, regardless of the season of the year. The Holy Spirit supernaturally inoculates my body.

8. I proclaim that my household will not experience the terror of terminal illness or the fear of evil arrows that waste at noonday. I destroy every thing that destroys in my

neighborhood by the power in His name.

9. According to the Word of the Lord, my feet are ushered to the place of greatness and lifting. I move with vision and precision. Clarity and the grace to fulfill my calling in destiny are available to me at all times in Jesus' name.

10. I will not die young in the mighty name of Jesus! I will live long to a ripe full age and I will see my children's children to the third and fourth generation in Jesus' name.

11. From today, because I am dwelling consciously under the shadow of the Almighty, demons begin to tremble at my command. I trample the serpents and scorpions under my feet.

12. My family is surrounded by angels at all times. The wall of fire hedges us in when we sleep and when we drive or fly, we ride on the chariots of fire. My children enjoy the protection of the Most High at all times.

Give thanks for answered prayers!

DAY 7
AVENGE ME SPEEDILY

Today is the seventh day of The Chosen Fast and seven is the number of rest. It represents perfection. It reflects complete and total fulfillment. It is the Sabbath day. I pray that you will enter your place of sweat-less and restful fulfillment.

The prayer call for today is AVENGE ME SPEEDILY! The Bible says that we have been called to a life of glory and virtue but a lot of us have been deprived and denied of glory. Some of our virtues have been stolen by the thief or caged in the stronghold of the adversary. After gaining understanding from this altar of prayer, I am assured that destinies will be restored because of Christ's redemptive plan.

As an individual, you have a purposeful destiny as ordained by God in Jeremiah 1:5. Before He formed you, He knew you and ordained you as something to your generation. If you also look closely at the scripture in 2 Peter 1:3, we see that we have a redemptive destiny in Christ Jesus that should be depicting the splendor of our King – His glory and majesty. What does glory mean? It means distinction, honor, magnificence and prosperity. It means the true essence of a thing. It can also be described as a state of achievement or full gratification. Virtue, on the other hand, means potency, power or the effective force of a thing – like the healing virtue of a particular herb is its potency. We also know that virtue is sometimes used to describe righteousness and chastity.

Is your life the opposite of the definition of glory and virtue? Or do you have some areas of victory and some areas outstanding? Then you must cry out today for complete restoration of your glory and virtue in Jesus' name. It is part of your redemptive heritage in Christ Jesus. Even though the devil claimed a right in the glory of man at the fall and tainted the glory, Christ died so we can have it back in full (John 10:10). We are taking it back in full and speedily too!

Numbers 27:1-11 - *Then came the daughters of Zelophehad the son of Hepher, the son of Gilead, the son of Machir, the son of Manasseh, from the families of Manasseh the son of Joseph; and these were the names of his daughters: Mahlah, Noah, Hoglah, Milcah, and Tirzah. And they stood before Moses, before Eleazar the priest, and before the leaders and all the congregation, by the doorway of the tabernacle of meeting, saying: "Our father died in the wilderness; but he was not in the company of those who gathered together against the Lord, in company with Korah, but he died in his own sin; and he had no sons. Why should the name of our father be removed from among his family because he had no son? Give us a possession among our father's brothers." So Moses brought their case before the Lord. And the Lord spoke to Moses, saying: "The daughters of Zelophehad speak what is right; you shall surely give them a possession of inheritance among their father's brothers, and cause the inheritance of their father to pass to them. And you shall speak to the children of Israel, saying: 'If a man dies and has no son, then you shall cause his inheritance to pass to his daughter. If he has no daughter, then you shall give his inheritance to his brothers. If he has no brothers, then you shall give his inheritance to his father's brothers. And if* *his father has no brothers, then you shall give his inheritance to the relative closest to him in his family, and he shall possess it.'" And it shall be to the children of Israel a statute of judgment, just as the Lord commanded Moses.*

Like the daughters of Zelophehad, we have come to ask for our rightful inheritance in Christ Jesus. In what area has the enemy robbed you? Is it in your career, marriage, academics, finances or health? We are going to cry out to the only wise Judge to avenge us speedily!

Jesus told a parable about a widow in Luke 18:1-3,5-8,

Then He spoke a parable to them, that men always ought to pray and not lose heart, saying: "There was in a certain city a judge who did not fear God nor regard man. Now there was a widow in that city; and she came to him, saying, 'Get justice for me from my adversary.' yet because this widow troubles me I will avenge her, lest by her continual coming she weary me.'" Then the Lord said, "Hear what the unjust judge said. And shall God not avenge His own elect who cry out day and night to Him, though He bears long with them? I tell you that He will avenge them speedily. Nevertheless, when the Son of Man comes, will He really find faith on the earth?"

Our God is better than any earthly judge. He is here on this prayer mountain to avenge you speedily because He is the controller of the times and seasons.

Psalm 94:1 - *O Lord God, to whom vengeance belongs—O God, to whom vengeance belongs, shine forth!*

The KJV says, "…show thyself!"

I proclaim that as you call on the Mighty Avenger for every outstanding situation, His divine timing will intercept every natural timing on your behalf in Jesus' mighty name. You are going to cry out to the holy and true Judge to avenge you speedily, like the saints in Revelation 6:10,

> *And they cried with a loud voice, saying, "How long, O Lord, holy and true, until You judge and avenge our blood on those who dwell on the earth?"*

We are also going be addressing the strongman who has all our goods in his stronghold, by telling him, "Give me my inheritance back! Give me my job back! Give me my marriage back! Give me my children back and return back everything you stole from me!" We are moving our inheritance out of the stronghold of the enemy to the rightful holding place in our possession.

Matthew 12:29 and Mark 3:27 both say the same thing:

> *Or how can one enter a strong man's house and plunder his goods, unless he first binds the strong man? And then he will plunder his house.*

It is time to disarm the satanic gatekeepers with the name that is higher than every other name. In Leviticus 6:4, the Bible says when a thief is caught, he must restore with extra but Proverbs 6:31 further says that when he is found, he must restore sevenfold; he may have to give up all the substance of his house. Are you ready for a speedy sevenfold return today? Then it is time to pray! It is time to demolish strongholds and breakdown walls to take back all that was ours in the first place.

DAY 7 PRAYER POINTS:

1. Thank You for calling me to a life of glory and virtue in Christ Jesus and making me a partaker of your divine nature in life and destiny.

2. Thank You for the grace and peace be multiplied to me in the knowledge of You and for the exceedingly great and precious promises given to me through redemption.

3. Thank You for my redemptive rights through the blood of Jesus shed on the cross of Calvary and for the Abrahamic order of blessings made available to me in Christ Jesus.

4. Thank You for being my Avenger and granting me insight to the secrets I need to take back all that the enemy has stolen from me. From today, I will no longer plant for another to eat or build for another to inhabit in Jesus' name.

5. O Lord God, to whom vengeance belongs - show Yourself in the issue of my marriage, academics, career, court case, finances, health, immigration status, family! Avenge me speedily like the daughters of Zelophehad - I possess my possessions! (*mention the specific areas before the Lord*).

6. Mighty God, rise up from the place of thunder and shatter every stronghold holding down my glory and virtue. I must enter my place of rich fulfillment before this year is over in Jesus' mighty name.

7. I break every yoke of ungodly delay and stagnation, sickness, poverty and marital affliction by the blood of Jesus! I receive the insight to enforce my redemptive victory over

every area of my life.

8. From today, I operate with distinction, honor and the magnificence of my King. The true essence of my life is released in Jesus' name. I have the power and full potency to make wealth and reach my full potential in life and ministry.

9. I bind every household demon or community idol that has stolen from my family and my generations past. I decree that every collective or individual captivity is broken in Jesus' name. I take back my virtue to achieve greatness in Christ Jesus.

10. I speak speedy turnaround for every situation that has defied solution and I command a seven-fold restoration of everything that the enemy has stolen from me in Jesus' name.

11. Consuming Fire, burn down any evil altar or stronghold holding down my blessings. I denounce every lawful captivity and I receive abundance for lack and double honor for every reproach. I decree a permanent turnaround for me and my household in Jesus' name.

12. From today I become an ambassador of the kingdom to set people free from every yoke of darkness and every oppression of the wicked. I am empowered to release people into their God-ordained destinies in Jesus' name.

Give thanks for answered prayers!

DAY 8
JUBILEE

Today is the eighth day of The Chosen Fast. The number 8 represents a new beginning. I pray that you will receive an opportunity from the Lord to start afresh and experience a new chapter in your life in Jesus' name.

In Genesis 8, the Lord gave Noah and his family a new beginning after the flood and the entire family was 8 in number. On this 8th day, you and your entire household will enter a season of new things and new beginnings in Jesus' name.

In this new beginning, God will replace every old thing in your life with a new one. You will shed that old skin for a new one and your youth will be renewed like that of Daniel and his friends after they had fasted.

Daniel 1:15 - *They appeared better and fairer in flesh that their peers.*

There will be divine displacement for kingdom replacement in your life like Esther. Every Vashti sitting on your throne will be supernaturally dethroned so you can take your rightful place in Jesus' mighty name. The Lord will usher you into divine locations and bring you into tender favor with kings.

You will experience divine connections that will lead to divine promotions in the name of Jesus. The Almighty will begin to raise destiny helpers and bring you into the presence of covenant friends that will impact your destiny positively. You will dine with royalty and learn at the feet of experts in your field. The Word says in Isaiah 49:23,

Kings shall be your foster fathers, and their queens your nursing mothers; They shall bow down to you with their faces to the earth, And lick up the dust of your feet. Then you will know that I am the Lord, for they shall not be ashamed who wait for Me."

In this new beginning, you will eat bread without scarceness and the Lord will bless your bread and your water. He will use you to display His glory as a signet ring according to Haggai 2:23.

In what area of your life do you desire a new beginning? Is it in your career, your marriage, your ministry or your health? God is ready to open that new chapter for you today. Are you saddled neck deep in debt that you have become a byword and a proverb? There is a release for a new beginning. The Lord will release you from that burden because Christ is the wisdom and the power of God unto us according to 1 Corinthians 1:24 and 30. He will draw you out from under that heavy burden through a miraculous intervention or by giving you a strategy to work your way out of that debt through His supernatural wisdom. It can be through power (miracle) or through wisdom (process). Either way, you are getting out to a clean start.

On this 8th day, let us a take a quick look at the concept of new beginnings written for the children of Israel in the book of Leviticus. These were written for our example and were truly a shadow of the real substance we have in Christ.

> **Leviticus 25:8-9** - *'And you shall count seven sabbaths of years for yourself, seven times seven years; and the time of the seven sabbaths of years shall be to you forty-nine years. Then you shall cause the trumpet of the Jubilee to sound on the tenth day of the seventh month; on the Day of Atonement you shall make the trumpet to sound throughout all your land.*

> **Leviticus 25:13** - *'In this Year of Jubilee, each of you shall return to his possession.*

You are returning to your possessions in the mighty name of Jesus.

Verses 18-22 (NLT) say,

> *If you want to live securely in the land, follow my decrees and obey my regulations. Then the land will yield large crops, and you will eat your fill and live securely in it. But you might ask, 'What will we eat during the seventh year, since we are not allowed to plant or harvest crops that year?' Be assured that I will send my blessing for you in the sixth year, so the land will produce a crop large enough for three years. When you plant your fields in the eighth year, you will still be eating from the large crop of the sixth year. In fact, you will still be eating from that large crop when the new crop is harvested in the ninth year.*

It is very clear from the scriptures above that there are times in life when we get stuck in the old and God bails us out with a new beginning. The Jubilee is God's bailout plan for His children. His plan is for you to return to your possession. What is it that you have lost? Today is a day of divine restoration! Are you stranded in that marriage? Call on the God of Jubilee today! Are you at your wits end in that academic pursuit? Call on the pathfinder and way-maker! Are you way over your head in debt like the widow of the prophet in 2 Kings 4:1-7, who became an oil merchant overnight?

Call on the God of new beginnings. Are you like one of the sons of the prophets in 2 Kings 6:5, who was cutting down a tree – the iron ax head fell into the water; and he cried out and said, "Alas, master! For it was borrowed." Have you drowned a major business capital in a failed project? Call on the God of Jubilee! If he did it before, He can do it again. Or are you like the woman with the issue of blood (Mark 5:26)? Come to the Great Physician today, He is waiting to heal you completely.

Are you at the brink of giving up or throwing in the towel about your marriage, children or career? Today is your day of new beginning as you step out in faith to accept the new beginning that God has ordained for you in the provision of the Jubilee; you will begin to jubilate forever in the Lord over that matter. We are sons of the prophet and called to be a royal priesthood after the order of Christ. We have a better covenant than the old and we have a higher calling than the Levitical priesthood.

Take your new beginning by faith as you make a list of all the areas that you need a touch. Apply the medicine of the Word and you will be amazed at the tremendous turnaround that will attract many people to follow you to your Helper – the God of Jubilee.

DAY 8 PRAYER POINTS:

1. Thank You Jesus for dying on the cross of Calvary and redeeming me from every outstanding debt of sin. Thank You for giving me a new beginning.

2. Thank You Lord for the mystery and revelation of the Jubilee of the Lord! Thank You for releasing me from the past and ushering me into a great future of new beginnings.

3. Thank You Heavenly Father for the power and wisdom of God available to us through salvation. Thank You for the blood of sprinkling that keeps speaking new beginning for me and everyone in my family.

4. Thank You for repairing every faulty foundation in life and bloodline through the blood of Jesus. Thank You for exchanging every heavy burdens with your burden for souls in my heart.

5. Father Lord, grant me a new beginning from this day forward in my finances, career, ministry...etc. I submit to your leading and instructions, and I tap into your grace to overcome at all times and in every situation. I operate with overcoming faith!

6. I lay every burden at Your feet Lord, I put on strength and praise as a garment. I leave every struggle and labor behind but choose to labor in the Word and the place of prayer to enter into Your rest. My bills are paid and my debts are written off in Jesus' name.

7. I speak to my situation right now (*mention it*). I receive

wisdom and power to enter into Jubilee. I possess my possession and take back all that I have lost in Jesus' name.

8. From today, I enjoy the favor of kings in my field of endeavor; kings foster me and their queens nurse me. I am ushered into the palace of kings and I make divine connections for exploits.

9. According to the Word of the Lord, I enter into a new beginning in my health; as I wait on the Lord my strength is renewed in Jesus' name. Every injured organ is repaired and every broken tissue is replaced. I speak divine restoration to any missing part of my body.

10. I recover every lost opportunity in life and past losses in my finances, career or timing. I speak to the four corners of the earth to release my divine helpers and I declare that strangers will build my walls and sons of foreigners will build my vineyards.

11. As I recover lost time and regain lost opportunities, I come in contact with great minds and covenant friends. I am a resource center and a solution carrier in all my endeavors. I am indispensable to the experts in my chosen field and career in Jesus' name. I am relevant to my generation!

12. I speak Jubilee to my marriage; my household will keep jubilating! I speak Jubilee to my church and ministry; we experience uncommon enlargement! I speak Jubilee to my work; my bread and my water are blessed! I speak Jubilee to my health; my health springs forth speedily!

Give thanks for answered prayers!

DAY 9
HONEY AND THE HONEYCOMB

This is the ninth day of The Chosen Fast. My prayer is that as you journey with the Holy Spirit in this fast, you will grow and manifest the nine fruits of the spirit as listed in Galatians 5:22. I pray that all the nine gifts of the spirit as listed in 1 Corinthians 12:7-10 will be fully at work in you, as the Lord wills. You will become a battle-ax in the hands of our King – an arrow in His mighty hands.

Today, we will be looking in depth at the concept of the honey and the honey-comb. Proverbs 24:13-14 says,

> *My son, eat honey because it is good, And the honeycomb which is sweet to your taste; So shall the knowledge of wisdom be to your soul; If you have found it, there is a prospect (reward), And your hope (expectation) will not be cut off* (Emphasis mine).

What is honey and what is the relevance of the honeycomb? Man is spirit, lives in a body and has a soul or mind (will, intellect and emotion). God is spirit and we are made in His image and after His likeness. There is physical food, bread or meat to feed the body with but that will not feed the spirit or soul; the spirit feeds on the Word of God. In the Bible the Word is referred to as milk for babes and honey for sons. The first time God introduced honey to man as a diet for spiritual walk was in Exodus 3:8,

> *So I have come down to deliver them out of the hand of the Egyptians, and to bring them up from that land to a good and large land, to a land flowing with milk and honey...*

Hebrews 5:12-13 also reiterates the same truth. For us to subdue the flesh and walk in the spirit we must feed our spirit man with adequate food. One type of food is the bread of life (Jesus Christ himself, through salvation and the Communion). Another type of food is the wine, representing the Holy Spirit and the blood of Jesus. Yet another type of food is meat representing the flesh of Jesus and the Word of God. The simplest form of food is the milk and curd or butter needed to feed babes; processed milk becomes curd or what is also known as butter.

Proverbs 30:33 - *For as the churning of milk produces butter...*

What does this churning or processing involve? Meditation is the processing of the Word or milk that a baby Christian consumes.

Honey represents sweetness and is known to have medicinal properties when used inwardly or applied outwardly. The honeycomb, on the other hand, is the holding house or the place where the honey is produced. All across scriptures, milk and honey are mentioned together as food for God's children. The psalmist in Psalm 119:103 said,

> *How sweet are Your words to my taste, Sweeter than honey to my mouth!*

The greatest love song ever written talks about honey in the mouth of the beloved:

Song of Solomon 4:11 - *Your lips, O my spouse,Drip as the honeycomb; Honey and milk are under your tongue; And the fragrance of your garments Is like the fragrance of Lebanon.*

Song of Solomon 5:1 - *I have come to my garden, my sister, my spouse;I have gathered my myrrh with my spice; I have eaten my honeycomb with my honey; I have drunk my wine with my milk. Eat, O friends! Drink, yes, drink deeply, O beloved ones!*

Honey refers to the Word of God in its raw form and the honeycomb represents the processing or meditation of the Word. For more details on how to study the Word, please go to my notes on facebook at Raeni Bankole and find Bible Study 101 (link: https://www.facebook.com/notes/raeni-bankole/bible-study-101/10151693013685963).

The honey and the honeycomb is further used to describe the efficacy of God's Word in Psalm 19:7-11. All through scriptures, God kept telling His people that He will feed them with milk and honey (e.g. Leviticus 20:24). And we know that their experience was a shadow of the substance we have in Christ Jesus. Lions eat honey (Judges 14:14, 18) and we are the children of the Lion of Judah!

See the following scriptures promoting the efficacy of the Word of God as medicinal tonic (Proverbs 3:8, Proverbs 4:22, Proverbs 16:24). The Word grants you the quickness and supernatural intelligence in warfare that can only be gotten from the Lord!

Hebrews 4:12 describes the Word of God as living and powerful, and sharper than any two-edged sword, piercing even to the division of soul and spirit, and of joints and marrow, and is a discerner of the thoughts and intents of the heart. The Word can flush out poison and cancer from the body of the consumer! Try it three times daily. There is no medicine as potent as the honey of His Words. Part of our spiritual artillery in battle is this Word (Ephesians 6:17).

When you eat the honey and the honeycomb, i.e. you study and meditate on the Word of God, you will bring the enemy cheaply to their knees. When you abide by this Word and feed on it, it builds you up with overcoming faith (1 John 5:2-5).

John the Baptist in his earthly ministry fed on honey too. He knew the Word of God thoroughly in order to be the fore-runner of the Messiah (see Mark 1:6-7).

You must consume the Word in large doses and swallow it whole – I promise you it has no side effect. I will also let you know that swallowing the Word without meditation or digesting it well can lead to constipation. Sometimes, it may be sweet in your mouth but bitter in your stomach like what John experienced in Revelation 10:10. Some truths are bitter but God will give you abundant grace to bear it. There are times when it will be to rebuke or chastise a person, family, church or nation. At such times, it is bitter but it will eventually bring out the best. In order to manifest His true nature, we must feed our spirit man with the honey and the honeycomb.

DAY 9 PRAYER POINTS:

1. Thank You dear Lord for the revelation of your Word as honey and the honeycomb. Thank You for Your words and commandments that are not grievous or burdensome for me to keep.

2. Thank You Holy Spirit for opening the eyes of my understanding to behold wondrous things out of the Word. Thank You for the water of the Word that purifies my conscience from dead works.

3. Thank You Jesus for giving me the keys of the kingdom through revelation in the knowledge of You, making me victorious over the gates of hell and death.

4. Thank You for the entrance of Your Word that gives light and understanding to the simple. Thank You for guiding me and lighting my path, keeping me from the power of sin through your Word (Psalm 119:103,105,130).

5. I lay aside all malice, strife and other works of the flesh as I feast daily at your table, drinking the milk and honey of your Word for my relationships at home and abroad. I display uncommon maturity as I study and meditate on Your Word.

6. As I study the Word of God daily, I display unequaled intelligence and supernatural wisdom to resolve problems quickly. I operate with crystallized and fluid intelligence and I manifest the excellent spirit of the Almighty at all times.

7. As an ambassador of the Kingdom and a minister of reconciliation, I know the right word to speak to him who

is weary and I have a word to answer when I evangelize. I study to show to myself approved, rightly dividing the Word of truth; I operate the sword of the spirit with dexterity in spiritual warfare.

8. As I locate the Word of God for my situation, I decree a thing and it is established and my prayer life moves to a new level. The Word of God becomes sweet to me and I rejoice as I discover treasures in the pages of scripture.

9. The Word of God is health to my flesh and strength to my bones in Jesus' name; the quality and length of my life increases as I study and meditate daily. My mortal body is quickened by the Rhema of the Word; my bones and marrow are renewed by the Spirit of the Most High.

10. As I delight myself in the honey of the Word day and night, I will be like a tree planted by the rivers of living water. I will produce fruits of success, good health, elevation, goodness and mercy in season; my leaf shall not wither and everything I do will prosper in Jesus' name (Psalm 1:2-3).

11. As I consume the Word (honey) and meditate daily (honeycomb), my life will release sweetness and attract many to the saving knowledge of our Lord Jesus Christ. I manifest son-ship as a lion. I will lay hands on the sick and they will recover and I will cast out demons effortlessly.

12. As I open the book of the law and meditate daily, my way is prosperous and I have good success. My household is blessed and my children are taught of the Lord. Our peace increases and we possess the land for our King.

Give thanks for answered prayers!

DAY 10
HE MADE THEM ONE

Today is the tenth day of The Chosen Fast. The number ten represents complete perfection and it represents divine order. My prayer today is that every missing area of your life will be supernaturally perfected and completely delivered unto you.

Today, in a caption tagged "He Made Them One", we will be looking closely at marriage as the Lord ordained it.

> **Malachi 2:15** - *But did He not make them one, Having a remnant of the Spirit? And why one? He seeks godly offspring. Therefore take heed to your spirit, And let none deal treacherously with the wife of his youth.*

Many people don't know the true purpose of marriage. God instituted marriage with a purpose and that purpose is to birth and nurture His seed or divine vision. The seed may be a physical one or a spiritual vision. For every marriage or family, there is a God-given mandate. A lot of people think marriage is made to cure loneliness and promote holiness - yes, but those are not all the reasons. The purpose of marriage far transcends curing loneliness; it is to fulfill a godly vision! Each individual in the home is the smallest unit and the home is God's smallest branch of the Kingdom. Several homes or families make up a church and several churches make part of His kingdom. When God looks at an individual or a home, He is actually seeing the church and His vast kingdom. This is why marriage is called a mystery that is patterned after Christ and His church (Ephesians 5:31-32).

Many believe marriage is for procreation solely i.e. having children, but that was not all that God had in mind. Let us go to the book of beginnings to see what God had in mind.

> **Genesis 1:27-28** - *So God created man in His own image; in the image of God He created him; male and female He created them. Then God blessed them, and God said to them, "Be fruitful and multiply; fill the earth and subdue it; have dominion over the fish of the sea, over the birds of the air, and over every living thing that moves on the earth."*

Many are fruitful but have not subdued the earth. Very few are walking in dominion and a number are still struggling with fruitfulness. Marriage is not only created for us to have a legitimate place intimacy, even though that is an essential part of it. He made marriage so that together with our spouses, our impact will be intensified and our power multiplied. The power and effect of a couple with unborn children is as strong as any family with children in it – that is the power of the marriage covenant! It is the power of unity; the power of oneness! Oneness in spirit, soul and body; the unity of vision and purpose!

When God looks at a couple or a family unit, He is seeing the mandate—His seed and His vision. There is something about that dysfunctional family that is still keeping God excited and He won't give up on them. Look through scriptures!

Regardless of the height of dysfunction, God still brings out His godly offspring, His seed and His vision.

Abraham and Sarah were attacked so much because of their godly seed but Isaac (the son of promise) was still born. Jacob and Rachel were attacked so much by the enemy, subverting their marital destiny with delay and barrenness, but eventually Joseph came to preserve their lives from famine. All through scriptures, when a great destiny is about to be born, chaos, delay, pandemonium and attacks abound!

Marriage is God's breeding ground for greatness. The family unit is His place to nurture His purpose, assignment and vision through godly seed(s)! Whether the devil likes it or not, your godly seed must be born! Regardless of the drama or dysfunction, He will fight for you! If you are single and have never been married, this is the best time to pray that you will fulfill heaven's mandate for your marital destiny. The void you feel as a single person is a proof that there is a true match out there for you. God is the greatest matchmaker. Rest in Him and trust Him completely. Stop fretting about it. Adam got Eve in a state of rest. There is a good, acceptable and perfect will of God for you in life out there – not three people but one – if you have really placed you life on the altar of sacrifice like Romans 12:1-2 says.

Having an understanding of God's purpose for marriage is very crucial. Make sure you pray for your children concerning their God-given purpose in marriage and destiny right from a young age. God has specific instructions on how to raise every child for their assignment. See the prayer of Samson's parents in Judges 13:8, 12,

Then Manoah prayed to the Lord, and said, "O my Lord, please let the Man of God whom You sent come to us again and teach us what we shall do for the child who will be born." Manoah said, "Now let Your words come to pass! What will be the boy's rule of life, and his work?"

The home is the first prayer and Word school for children. Parents are custodians of children (they really belong to God) and they are to raise them to fulfill their assignment and great destinies in Christ (Psalm 127:3-5).

If your marriage is rocky, you can pray it back into God's divine order on this tenth day of The Chosen Fast. You can intercede for that unbelieving spouse. Even if you are thinking right now, "What if I married the wrong person?" or "...I am a second or third wife." God will give you abundant grace to still bring out His desired seed. Remember David came out of a polygamous home, Jephthah as well and so did Joseph. Please keep praying for His will to be done in your life. From today, I speak peace to your home and rest to that chaos in Jesus' name.

Finally, some people will still fulfill God's vision for their lives without marriage, like Paul or Daniel who were never married. These are rare and far between but in most situations when an individual who is not saved does not feel an attraction to the opposite sex, the devil may pervert such destinies with being gay. Please celebrate your celibacy in Christ and fulfill your godly vision in Jesus' name. Know that there is nothing wrong with you if you have this gift to help you serve the Lord without any distraction, like Paul (1 Corinthians 7:7-9, 32-33). Whether single or married you are God's offspring and His vision according to Malachi 2:15. You are complete in Him!

Pray that you fulfill that mandate today as an individual and as a family.

DAY 10 PRAYER POINTS:

1. Thank You heavenly Father for this prayer altar; for Your spirit of revelation unfolding the mysteries of marriage and the purpose of family. Thank You for healing virtue available to heal my family.

2. Thank You for loving me with an everlasting love and rejoicing over me as a bridegroom rejoices over his bride. Thank You for entering a new covenant with me through the blood of Jesus.

3. Thank You for the great marriage supper that I look forward to at the close of this age and the grace to be a partaker of the new life available through the finished work of Christ on the cross.

4. Thank You for that vision (godly seed) that you see in me that keeps You excited about me, despite my mess-ups and slip-ups. Thank You for not giving up on me or my family.

5. O God, settle every outstanding matter in my marital destiny. Turn every delay around with divine speed and replace every reproach with Your double honor. *Mention your specific situation before Him.*

6. Lord, before this year is over, visit my foundation and repair my past from any evil trend. Heal my pain and erase any shame in Jesus' name. Fulfill Your purpose concerning me, according to Psalm 20:4.

7. My marital destiny must fulfill divine mandate and my family must comply with divine order in Jesus' name. Silence every controversial noise in my home. Restore broken homes and heal broken hearts (Ezekiel 37:7).

8. My husband and I will raise our children together as the Lord ordained it. No weapon formed against us shall prosper. Every conspiracy against our divine purpose is shattered by the blood of Jesus! (Isaiah 54:13-14,17).

9. Our home is a tension-free zone filled with the peace of God that passes all human understanding. People who visit our home enjoy peace and our home is a lighthouse to the darkness of this world.

10. Lord, grant me restoration of all lost years in love and intimacy by the blood of Jesus! Our love is renewed and our covenant is deepened in Jesus' name. Destroy any evil personality attacking my home and break every ungodly soul-tie in Jesus' name.

11. I destroy every influence of a third party in my marriage in Jesus' name. We walk in agreement in our visions and purposes; our individual visions complement one another. We hear each other out when we talk and we are in complete agreement when we pray.

12. I prophesy that our relationship gets better and our friendship grows deeper. Our marriage becomes sweeter and our love deepens intimately. Every godly seed bears fruit in our home and we will fulfill our God-given mandate in Jesus' name.

Give thanks for answered prayers!

DAY 11
ELEVENTH HOUR MIRACLE

Today is the eleventh day of The Chosen Fast journey and it is a day of eleventh hour miracles. Has the doctor given you a sudden report that only an instant miracle can change? Receive your miracle now in Jesus' name! Has your school given you a deadline that only God can meet up with? Have you been struggling endlessly with a persistent problem that you are almost giving up on yourself? Take your eleventh hour miracle right now! He can show up when no one can and He can raise the dead from the mortuary! He can turn the verdict of surgeons to nothing and He can defeat strange battles without lifting a finger.

What is the eleventh hour miracle? We all know that the old day hands over to a new day at 12 midnight and an old month hands over to a new month at 12 midnight, so also a New Year hands over to a new year at 12 midnight without fail. I want to let you know that from this eleventh day of The Chosen Fast and for the remaining days of your life, you will experience a barrage of eleventh hour miracles on a daily basis.

The eleventh hour miracle is the blessing you get even when you don't deserve it. It is an opportunity to catch up with those who have gone ahead of you. Let us look at the instance where the term *eleventh hour* was used in the Bible:

Matthew 20:1-12,16 - *"For the kingdom of heaven is like a landowner who went out early in the morning to hire laborers for his vineyard. Now when he had agreed with the laborers for a denarius a day, he sent them into his vineyard. And he went out about the third hour and saw others standing idle in the marketplace, and said to them, 'You also go into the vineyard, and whatever is right I will give you.' So they went. Again he went out about the sixth and the ninth hour, and did likewise. And about the eleventh hour he went out and found others standing idle, and said to them, 'Why have you been standing here idle all day?' They said to him, 'Because no one hired us.' He said to them, 'You also go into the vineyard, and whatever is right you will receive.' "So when evening had come, the owner of the vineyard said to his steward, 'Call the laborers and give them their wages, beginning with the last to the first.' And when those came who were hired about the eleventh hour, they each received a denarius. But when the first came, they supposed that they would receive more; and they likewise received each a denarius. And when they had received it, they complained against the landowner, saying, 'These last men have worked only one hour, and you made them equal to us who have borne the burden and the heat of the day.' So the last will be first, and the first last. For many are called, but few chosen."*

The passage is self-explanatory; I want you know that The Lord of eleventh hour miracles will break protocol for you! Have you been jobless for a while that you think no one will hire you? God is about to bring you to a place of overwhelming and heart-warming promotion! You will receive pay back for all that the devil stole from you. You will be paid in arrears in cash and in kind! If all your mates have gotten married and there is no one left for you to be their bridesmaid, you will get that long awaited miracle husband in Jesus' name. Every diabolical chain of delay is broken over your life. The fire of the Holy Ghost roasts that evil veil of covering on your head. Those who have been waiting to conceive their own children, receive the strength to conceive and the power to carry your children to full term. You will become a joyful mother of children. The Lord will grant you laughter and people will gather to celebrate with you according to the time of life in Jesus' name!

Today, we will be looking closely at the story of Joseph, the eleventh son of Jacob. What were the major things that were reflective in his life? His birth was delayed, his mother died when he was young, he was hated by his brothers, he had big dreams that looked like they would never come to pass, he was thrown in a pit, he was stripped naked and had his robe torn to shreds, he was sold out to slavery, he was wrongfully accused and went to prison for years for a sin he never committed. Can you identify with this lad? But his story did not end there! He went from the pit to Potiphar's house, from slavery to prison – it looked as if his fortune took a turn for the worse but wait! He went from sleeping in the prison one night to waking up in the palace the next morning. God took a little boy from slavery to primacy! God took him from zero to hero and took him from a forgotten place to a place of remembrance.

Do you feel like you have been constantly bypassed from promotions or blessings? Or you have experienced unexplainable hatred from those who should be helping or loving you? Today, through the mystery of the eleventh hour miracle, you will experience your turnaround!

His dream started in Genesis 37:3-8. He shared the dream with his family and his brothers despised him and sold him into slavery. From deep hatred to the pit of slavery; from the pit to the palace; from the palace to the prison. It seemed like his dream would not come to pass. But one day, his story changed!

> **Genesis 41:1, 39-45** - *Then it came to pass, at the end of two full years, that Pharaoh had a dream; and behold, he stood by the river. Then Pharaoh said to Joseph, "Inasmuch as God has shown you all this, there is no one as discerning and wise as you. You shall be over my house, and all my people shall be ruled according to your word; only in regard to the throne will I be greater than you." And Pharaoh said to Joseph, "See, I have set you over all the land of Egypt." Then Pharaoh took his signet ring off his hand and put it on Joseph's hand; and he clothed him in garments of fine linen and put a gold chain around his neck. And he had him ride in the second chariot which he had; and they cried out before him, "Bow the knee!" So he set him over all the land of Egypt. Pharaoh also said to Joseph, "I am Pharaoh, and without your consent no man may lift his hand or foot in all the land of Egypt." And Pharaoh called Joseph's name Zaphnath-Paaneah. And he gave him as a wife Asenath, the daughter of Poti-Pherah priest of On. So Joseph went out over all the land of Egypt.*

Joseph obtained double honor, double promotion; his marital destiny was restored; he obtained authority and attained primacy!

Your toiling has come to an end – it is approaching its midnight hour! This is the eleventh hour; what do you want? What have you not seen yet? What have you been denied of? What opportunities have you lost? What deadlines have you missed? Take it all back today (with interest) at the altar of eleventh hour miracles!

DAY 11 PRAYER POINTS:

1. Thank You Lord for the enduring mercy and grace to be a partaker of the inheritance of the saints in Christ Jesus. Thanks for redeeming me through the blood of Jesus (Colossians 1:12-14).

2. Thank You Father for being such a faithful employer, rewarding each one of us with an inheritance that we could never earn by our own ability or power (Colossians 3:23-24).

3. Thank You Lord for the grace to be a co-laborer in your vineyard knowing full well that my labor is not in vain, now and hereafter.

4. Thank You for the gift of life, family and good health. Thank You for shelter and provision. Thank You for safety and protection over my entire household.

5. God of eleventh hour miracles, move my case from the back to the forefront. From today, I leave the realm of the least to the greatest and I vacate the place of zero to hero in Jesus' name. I move from the valley to the top!

6. Crown this year with a chain of eleventh hour miracles for my entire household and me. Give us individual and generational payback for denied blessings! Give me my job, my child, my robe of honor, my honor and dignity, my glory and virtue!

7. Just as an old year never returns, turn around my captivity like the rushing streams of the south that cannot be turned back – Sickness must go, poverty must leave, toiling must go

and struggling must stop in Jesus' name.

8. I open my arms to receive all my outstanding blessings due to me and my family this year; I take my promotion, I receive double honor, I move forward with uncommon speed and I recover every lost profit and opportunities in Jesus' name.

9. Like Joseph, I take back my wealth and enjoy my lifting in good health. My name is constantly on the lips of kings and my destiny helpers will begin to recommend me for greatness.

10. Father Lord, I intercede on behalf of my father's house. Like Joseph, we will encounter Goshen. We will move from least to the greatest; make us a household name like the house of David!

11. Dream Giver, restore all my stolen dreams and destroy every household wickedness that is tying me down to the same spot. I break the yoke of stagnation and receive divine acceleration at the altar of eleventh hour miracles.

12. Mention the area you need God's speedy intervention before this year is over! Hannah got her instant miracle at the altar for fruitfulness. Father, let all those who gathered to laugh at me gather together to laugh with me concerning my job, my health, my children, my marriage, my destiny, my ministry, my immigration papers etc.

Give thanks for answered prayers!

DAY 12
HEALING OF THE NATIONS

Today is the twelveth day of The Chosen Fast. The number twelve is very significant – we have 12 hours from midnight to noon and another 12 hours from noon to midnight. We also have 12 months in a year. There are twelve tribes of Israel and twelve disciples of our Lord Jesus Christ. Twelve represents *Chronos* as well as *Kairos* timing (see Revelations 22:2). Chronos is the physical timing that you can track on the clock while Kairos is the appointed time in the purposes of God – the opportune time, the supreme moment – and it is tracked in Heaven. It is that sweet moment when divine timing coincides with or overrides physical timing.

My prayer today is that the Almighty God who controls the times and the seasons will move mightily on your behalf over that slow situation and make it swift in Jesus' name. Receive the grace to operate by divine timing and not only physical timing from this day forward!

The number 12 also represents divine government. Let us briefly examine Revelation 22:1-2,

And he showed me a pure river of water of life, clear as crystal, proceeding from the throne of God and of the Lamb. In the middle of its street, and on either side of the river, was the tree

of life, which bore twelve fruits, each tree yielding its fruit every month. The leaves of the tree were for the healing of the nations.

Today, we are focusing on the leaves of that tree in heaven that is meant for the healing of the nations. You are going to pray for the healing of your nation! What is your nation of origin or the nation where you reside? Both need your prayer. God is looking for an intercessor, a man who will stand in the gap to pray His will to fruition and His Kingdom to manifestation on planet earth. He is looking for those whose hearts are connected to His purpose to show Himself mighty on their behalf. He is waiting for His people called by His name to pray.

> **2 Chronicles 16:9** - *For the eyes of the Lord run to and fro throughout the whole earth, to show Himself strong on behalf of those whose heart is loyal to Him.*

In 2 Chronicles 7:14-16 He said,

> *If My people who are called by My name will humble themselves, and pray and seek My face, and turn from their wicked ways, then I will hear from heaven, and will forgive their sin and heal their land. Now My eyes will be open and My ears attentive to prayer made in this place. For now I have chosen and sanctified this house, that My name may be there forever; and My eyes and My heart will be there perpetually.*

God strategically planted you in that location, nation and this generation for a purpose. Like Esther, the Bible said that you were born for such a time as this but if you refuse, God will find a replacement (Esther 4:13-14). We can see how God used Esther and Mordecai to change the constitution of the land through prayer and fasting. You cannot fold your hands and watch things depreciate into decadence in your nation. Whether you live there or not! You may say, "This is not my country; when all is said and done, I will go back home." But when last did you pray for your "home"? We are meant to pray for our countries of origin and residence. God is calling on you now.

God promised in Joshua 1:3 that every place that the soles of your foot will tread upon He will give you. When you fight for a land, you own it.

Joshua 24:13 - *I have given you a land for which you did not labor, and cities which you did not build, and you dwell in them; you eat of the vineyards and olive groves which you did not plant.*

Like Joshua and Daniel, God is looking for warriors to defeat territorial darkness.

Daniel was a watchman for the nation of Israel. He prayed so much for the nation that secrets were revealed to him and angels were appearing to him regularly! Please read Daniel 9 & 10 in your spare time to see how he was praying and fasting and God was revealing secrets to him about nations, generations and future eras. He didn't attain that in one day. In chapter one, he fasted for himself and excelled. In chapter two, he fasted and prayed for the king with his friends and got promoted. In chapter three, his friends got in a super-size oven but were still unstoppable. In chapter six, he kept praying and landed in the lions' den. He suppressed territorial darkness like the Prince of Persia and he outlived four (4) kings, subduing nations and impacting generations.

You must pray for your neighborhood day and night, till testimonies break forth.

> **Isaiah 62:6-7** - *I have set watchmen on your walls, O Jerusalem; They shall never hold their peace day or night -keep silent, And give Him no rest till He makes Jerusalem a praise in the earth.*

He planted you there for a purpose (Ezekiel 33:7). Nothing should happen without you having an idea from the Lord, like Abraham in Genesis 18:17-23. You must pray for God's will to prevail over the government of your land.

> **Isaiah 60:17b-18** - *I will also make your officers peace,And your magistrates righteousness. Violence shall no longer be heard in your land,Neither wasting nor destruction within your borders; But you shall call your walls Salvation,And your gates Praise.*

Many of us feel we have outgrown our present location or nation and we want to move to a new house or state. But we haven't completed our divine assignments in our current locations. You want to cut the journey short; but until you touch that life, save that soul or pray that city through, you may be stuck there for a while. You must pray all those in your building into the kingdom, then proceed to pray for those in your block, city, state, nation and even your generation.

In order to set Kairos time in motion, start using your Chronos time well in prayer. Observe the prayer watches (not selfishly, but praying for those people in your neighborhood that don't even know your name). There is a tremendous blessing loaded in the land, but you must first fulfill the intercessory part of the deal.

DAY 12 PRAYER POINTS:

1. Thank You Lord for the divine calling I have in you as a lawgiver in the order of Judah and the Root of Jesse. Thank You for the scepter of rulership I have through salvation.

2. Thank You Father for calling me as a chosen generation and a royal priesthood to enforce your will on the earth. I am eternally grateful for making me a holy nation through the mercy available by Christ Jesus (1 Peter 2:9-10).

3. Thank You for calling me your friend like Abraham and telling me of things before they happen in my location, nation and generation in the place of prayer.

4. Thank You Father for the depth of revelation you are showing me on this altar. I am forever grateful because I know my life will not remain the same.

5. Father Lord, I receive the grace to intercede for my nation and generation like Daniel. I decree that constitutions will be rewritten; righteousness will exalt my city, state, nation (mention the name before the Lord). Violence will longer be heard in my land neither wasting nor destruction within our borders, according to Isaiah 60:18.

6. Deliver our leaders in government from the spirit of error and destroy every evil counsel/counselor. I pray that our officers will be peace and our exactors, righteousness.

7. We dethrone the rulers of darkness and the spirit of Ahab ruling in the presidency, congress or senate, state or local agencies including the judicial seats of power in Jesus' name.

We overthrow evil altars and pray that righteousness, peace and joy reign in our land.

8. Let churches everywhere catch the vision of praying for all nations; let the healing virtues from the tree of life in Revelation 22:2 be delivered through the prayers of the saints. You said if your people call, You will heal our land!

9. My household shall grow in the mandate of the Lord for our location and we will run with the vision of our King. As we align with divine vision in prayer, provision is made available to us without measure in Jesus' name.

10. My time for favor has come. As I intercede for the healing of the nations, gates of different nations begin to open before me and I enjoy the wealth of nations. In every place I have been rejected before now, they will begin to send for me. I am an eternal excellency and a joy to many generations.

11. According to Isaiah 60:17, there is a divine improvement of God upon everything I do in my school, work and ministry. As an intercessor, I possess the land where I live and I begin to inherit lands I did not labor for and cities I did not build. I will dwell in them in safety, eating vineyards and olive groves that I did not plant.

12. I am relevant in my generation for impact. When they mention ten people in my generation, my name will be at the top. My family is known for exploits and my children for signs and wonders in Jesus' name!

Give thanks for answered prayers!

DAY 13
SIGNS AND WONDERS

Today is the thirteenth day of The Chosen Fast. The Bible shows that it took Abraham thirteen years (between age 86-99) for the promise of having his son, Isaac, to manifest. I pray that you begin to experience fulfillment and manifestation of promises from this day forward in Jesus' name.

The topic of meditation today is **Signs and Wonders**. Children are for signs and wonders.

> **Isaiah 8:18** - *That I and the children whom the Lord has given me! We are for signs and wonders in Israel From the Lord of hosts, Who dwells in Mount Zion".*

God's purpose for the home is made very clear in the Bible. Look at what God said about Abraham in Genesis 18:19,

> *For I have known him, in order that he may command his children and his household after him, that they keep the way of the Lord, to do righteousness and justice, that the Lord may bring to Abraham what He has spoken to him.*

God ordained the home to be the first prayer and Bible study school our children will attend. If you do not have a family altar in your home where you pray with your children, please create one. And if you are not yet a parent, but still live at home with your parents, you can start one too. God desires to inhabit every heart and every altar in the home.

God wants our children hardwired by His Word; He wants us to raise godly children for His glory. The outcome is tremendous because godly families will make godly communities and eventually godly nations and generations and the cycle continues that way i.e. building holiness and righteousness from the nucleus out. The popular saying that charity begins at home is so true.

Many are so busy chasing the daily bread that they miss out on the purpose of God for raising a family with godly children. Proverbs 22:6 says we should, *"train up a child in the way he should go, and when he is old he will not depart from it."* The responsibility of raising children is not for the schoolteachers or the Sunday school class teacher, but for parents. Parents are the primary custodians of the great destinies that God gave them.

> **Deuteronomy 6:5-7** - *You shall love the Lord your God with all your heart, with all your soul, and with all your strength. "And these words which I command you today shall be in your heart. You shall teach them diligently to your children, and shall talk of them when you sit in your house, when you walk by the way, when you lie down, and when you rise up.*

I have personally noticed that children raised in homes saturated with prayer are usually peaceful and even tempered as in Isaiah 54:13,

> *All your children shall be taught by the Lord, And great shall be the peace of your children.*

Have you left children to their own devices by leaving them to be raised by baby sitters or the mass media and you wonder why they are not following in your God-fearing steps? The time to change is now! My prayer is that our children will not become prodigals under our watch in Jesus' name. We will not labor in vain over them according to Isaiah 65:23,

> *They shall not labor in vain, Nor bring forth children for trouble; For they shall be the descendants of the blessed of the Lord, And their offspring with them.*

If there is any child who has strayed from the path of righteousness, I declare that they will come back home like the prodigal son (Luke 15:17-18).

It is very important for parents to realize that each child is different in purpose and assignment. They have different temperaments, behaviors and emotions. It is totally unfair to treat every child the same way because there is a reason for their uniqueness. Each child has an assigned destiny from heaven (Jeremiah 1:5) and parents must pray their children into their God-given destiny and raise them according to divine instructions.

Samson's parents knew he was a different child and asked for help to know how to raise him in Judges 13:8,

> *Then Manoah prayed to the Lord, and said, "O my Lord, please let the Man of God whom You sent come to us again and teach us what we shall do for the child who will be born."*

Your children are not yours; you are just custodians to help guide them in their journeys to destiny.

Psalm 127:3-5 - *Behold, children are a heritage from the Lord, The fruit of the womb is a reward. Like arrows in the hand of a warrior, So are the children of one's youth. Happy is the man who has his quiver full of them; They shall not be ashamed, But shall speak with their enemies in the gate.*

There is a godly pattern that God ordained in scriptures for our children to follow - Samuel, John the Baptist and Jesus followed it (1 Samuel 2:26, Luke 1:80, Luke 2:40). They grew in wisdom and grace and in all aspects (spirit, soul and body). Start praying for the children to follow this pattern and there is no way they will not manifest to their world as signs and wonders in Jesus' name.

It is also very important for parents to pray Psalm 144 over their children to destroy every peer pressure and territorial influence. It is extremely powerful and precise for that purpose:

Psalm 144:7-8, 11-15 - *Stretch out Your hand from above; Rescue me and deliver me out of great waters, From the hand of foreigners, Whose mouth speaks lying words, And whose right hand is a right hand of falsehood. Rescue me and deliver me from the hand of foreigners, Whose mouth speaks lying words, And whose right hand is a right hand of falsehood— That our sons may be as plants grown up in their youth; That our daughters may be as pillars, Sculptured in palace style; That our barns may be full, Supplying all kinds of produce; That our sheep may bring forth thousands And ten thousands in our fields; That our oxen may be well laden; That there be no breaking in or going out; That there be no outcry in our streets. Happy are the people who are in such a state; Happy are the people whose God is the Lord!*

DAY 13 PRAYER POINTS:

1. Thank You Lord for making me Your child and for accepting me to the best family that could ever be, through the adoption of sons by Christ Jesus (Ephesians 1:5-6).

2. Thank You for giving me a physical family on planet earth. I am grateful for my birth parents, foster parents and spiritual parents. Thank You for my family of orientation and my family of procreation.

3. Thank You for children that are a heritage from You and for granting us access into Your divine will and purpose for raising a godly home. Thank You for making us a sign and a wonder to our world.

4. Thank You because my children will not struggle where I struggled. Father, I also thank you for the grace available to me as a parent to raise my children in the fear and nurture of the Lord and for the wisdom not to frustrate them.

5. Father Lord, perfect all that concerns our babies inside and outside the womb. I dedicate them, their lives, their goals, their careers and their choices to You. Their destinies shall not be cut off; they will fulfill scripture.

6. I receive strength and the power to raise children that are beautiful inside out, passionate for the Lord and consumed by His zeal in Jesus' name. Father, grant my spouse and I the wisdom and grace to raise our children according to divine instruction. Let them be well rounded for your glory.

7. My children will be as tender plants fully grown in their

youths displaying unequaled wisdom and maturity like Samuel. They will influence their generation for Christ and they shall be taught by the Lord and great shall be their peace.

8. In righteousness they shall be established and far from oppression, they will not fear the terror of terminal sicknesses and common diseases in Jesus' name. No weapon fashioned against them shall prosper including generational battles and untimely death.

9. My children will maintain honors roll like Daniel and command the scholarship of kings all through their schooling. They will worship God in purity and experience generational purity and blessings in Jesus' name.

10. I come against every spirit of near-success; failure at the edge of success will not be their portion. They receive the grace of a completer in all that they do and will operate with a mark of distinction.

11. Let them compel the favor of kings like Daniel; give them uncommon favor for Academic excellence. Release the spirit of excellence on our children. Grant them understanding and superior intelligence that commands scholarships (Daniel 1:4,20 KJV).

12. Deliver them from evil influence and from strange children. Restore all prodigal sons; let them find their way back home and find forgiveness! Soften the heart of rebellious children; put an end to strife and discord at home. Rid them of all evil like kidnap, perversion, sodomy, homosexuality, defiance and the corruption of the media by the blood of Jesus.

Give thanks for answered prayers!

DAY 14
CANDLE OF THE LORD

Today is the fourteenth day of The Chosen Fast. I pray that the Almighty God will manifest Himself to you on this altar in the name of Jesus. The number 14 represents double perfection. You will enter into your season of double perfection in Jesus' name.

One way to enjoy double perfection is to walk in the light of The Almighty. What do I mean by His light? I mean by His spirit and His Word.

Proverbs 20:27 - *The spirit of man is the candle of the Lord searching every inward parts of the belly.*

Job was a man that operated with an excellent spirit and he attested to this light in Job 29:3 (KJV),

When his candle shined upon my head, and when by his light I walked through darkness.

Job 32:8 also declares that there is a spirit in man and the inspiration of the Almighty gives him understanding. There is an excellence that exudes from a man that God indwells. This inspiration allows you to operate at a higher level than the elderly and intellectuals (Job 32:7-9, Psalm 119:98-100).

This spirit is the flame that lights the candle in man and allows an individual to operate with a different spirit. The Bible sometimes describes this phenomena as the seven spirits of God listed Isaiah 11:2-3,

> *²And the spirit of the LORD shall rest upon him, the spirit of wisdom and understanding, the spirit of counsel and might, the spirit of knowledge and of the fear of the LORD; ³And shall make him of quick understanding in the fear of the LORD: and he shall not judge after the sight of his eyes, neither reprove after the hearing of his ears.*

As a student, the inspiration of the almighty will grant you supernatural intelligence for academic excellence like Daniel and his friends (Daniel 1:4). I want to let you know that if you have this kind of inspiration and understanding like Daniel did, you can operate in the courts and palaces of kings; you can operate in the oval offices of presidents and governors; the experts in your field will begin to search for you. In Daniel 1:19-20, the Bible says the king interviewed the Hebrew boys and in all matters of wisdom and understanding and he found them to be ten times better than all the magicians and astrologers that were in all his realm.

This excellent spirit makes you smarter than your professors. This is the spirit that allows you to excel before panel of interviewers and causes you to excel in any professional exam that you write. Have you been struggling with a particular certification? Receive divine help today in Jesus' name. Today, through prayer, you will draw out this spirit of understanding. The Bible says in verse 12 that the hearing ears and the seeing eyes both belong to the Lord, so you are going to ask Him who has both of them to give them to you today in Jesus' name. There is a way to draw out this counsel and excellent spirit – it is through intense prayer and supplication especially in the spirit because Roman 8:26-27 says,

> [26]*Likewise the Spirit also helps in our weaknesses. For we do not know what we should pray for as we ought, but the Spirit Himself makes intercession for us with groanings which cannot be uttered.* [27]*Now He who searches the hearts knows what the mind of the Spirit is, because He makes intercession for the saints according to the will of God.*

When you pray in the spirit, you charge yourself up, stirring yourself up like a spiritual battery or a power house (Jude 1:20). The Holy Spirit is the Helper that the Lord told the disciples about in John 14:26. In other words, the Holy Ghost will show us things through picture-like visions, opening the eyes of your mind and your understanding will be enlightened. The Holy Ghost is the flame that ignites your candle and fuels your spirit for continuous exploits. He will trigger your imagination and inspire you with creative prowess. Imagination is the power to form mental pictures and it is also known as image formation. Positive imagination is creative thinking; creative thinking is the ability to conceive or birth an idea. The process or power of forming mental pictures will become evidently extraordinary in you.

I declare that wrong or depressive thinking and negative imaginations are destroyed from your life and replaced with positive ones in the name of Jesus (2 Corinthians 10:5). His light will speed up your thought process like the speed of light. What is it that you picture today? What is that positive imagination you have? If you can see it, you can have it! If only you can yield to the Holy Spirit to light the candle within you with His fire, you will begin to unlock all the secrets of the Most High locked away in the inner recesses of your spirit man. You will start to operate in the class of God Almighty and His intelligence. 1 Corinthians 2:9-16 says,

> [9]*But as it is written: "Eye has not seen, nor ear heard, Nor have entered into the heart of man the things which God has prepared for those who love Him."* [10]*But God has revealed them to us through His Spirit. For the Spirit searches all things, yes, the deep things of God.* [11]*For what man knows the things of a man except the spirit of the man which is in him? Even so no one knows the things of God except the Spirit of God.* [12]*Now we have received, not the spirit of the world, but the Spirit who is from God, that we might know the things that have been freely given to us by God.* [13]*These things we also speak, not in words which man's wisdom teaches but which the Holy Spirit teaches, comparing spiritual things with spiritual.* [14]*But the natural man does not receive the things of the Spirit of God, for they are foolishness to him; nor can he know them, because they are spiritually discerned.* [15]*But he who is spiritual judges all things, yet he himself is rightly judged by no one.* [16]*For "who has known the mind of the LORD that he may instruct Him?" But we have the mind of Christ.*

It is an awesome privilege to have access to this higher dimension of wisdom and operate with the excellent mind of the Creator. In case you have struggled with confusion or memory lapses, from today your mind is quickened in the order of the Most High! That difficult situation will receive speedy solution as you exercise the mind of Christ while praying in the spirit. Dark riddles will become very clear to you and you will begin to interpret dreams like Joseph and Daniel. You will begin to operate with the same spirit of excellence as our Lord Jesus Christ from this day forward.

DAY 14 PRAYER POINTS:

1. Thank You Lord for the spirit of wisdom and revelation in the knowledge of you, causing the eyes of my understanding to be enlightened and helping me to know the hope of my calling in Christ Jesus.

2. Thank You Lord for bringing us to the 14th day of the chosen fast and for renewing my strength supernaturally for the fulfillment of divine purpose. Thank You Lord for lighting my candle by your fire.

3. Thank You Lord for the healing power in the blood of Jesus that has removed all dullness from my mind and purged me of every psychological disorder. Thank You Lord for the fire of the Holy Ghost igniting your nature deep within me.

4. Thank You Lord for the Spirit that raised Christ from the dead that quickens my mind to operate in the school of the supernatural. Thank You Lord for baptizing me with the seven spirits of excellence according to Isaiah 11:2.

5. Father Lord, I receive a fresh baptism of your spirit that causes me to be ten times better than my peers in every interview panel I face and every exam I write. Thank You Lord for the excellent spirit that brings me before royalty.

6. From today, I begin to demonstrate the supernatural intelligence of God and I manifest the creative power of the Almighty. I have the ability to solve difficult problems and interpret dreams/riddles.

7. Like Daniel and his friends, let me begin to display uncommon abilities in science. I am gifted in all wisdom, I possess knowledge and I am quick to understand complex matters at work and in school.

8. Father, from Your light deep within me, I begin to navigate with ease through difficult situations. I operate with vision and precision. Your friendly counsel guides me to treasures and I enjoy the hidden riches from secret places.

9. In my career, ministry, academics and business, I walk in the wisdom and the knowledge of creative inventions. I compel the attention of the experts in my field.

10. From today, my prayer life takes a new turn and I step into a new dimension. I activate the seeing eyes and the hearing ears as I pray more intensely in the Spirit.

11. Father Lord, increase the intensity of Your light within me so that I can see in the realm of the invisible and hear into the realm of the inaudible. Give me the hearing ears of Samuel and the seeing eyes of Elisha. Speak to me face-to-face like Moses and anoint my tongue with fire like Elijah.

12. Father Lord, anoint me with fresh oil to be a solution carrier to my nation and generation. Enlarge my binocular and peripheral vision for Kingdom expansion. Grant me retentive memory and uncommon insight in Your Word.

Give thanks for answered prayers!

DAY 15
PRAY UNTIL SOMETHING HAPPENS (PUSH)

Today is the fifteenth day of The Chosen Fast. The Lord added 15 years to the life of King Hezekiah at the moment of devastation. Today, not only will the Lord add years to your life, He will add life to your years in Jesus' name. The Almighty God will restore to you all the years that the cankerworm, caterpillar and locust have eaten.

Today, we will be looking at the topic tagged **PUSH**, meaning **P**ray **U**ntil **S**omething **H**appens. There was a man named Jacob in the Bible. He needed another chance in life, so he went alone before the Lord all night and emerged a winner before the morning light, with a new name and a brand new life. Jesus speaking in Luke 18:1 said, *"men ought to always pray and not faint."* The Bible says in 1 Thessalonians 5:17, *"pray without ceasing."* As a believer, it is crucial to persevere in the place of prayer; you must not give up before your testimony is full. The Word of God says we should add perseverance to our faith (2 Peter 1:5-6).

While waiting, you must keep praying earnestly; that is the true sign that you are not giving up! The more the situation looks bleak, the more the need to intensify your prayers. It gets darkest just before dawn. I will also suggest that you to utilize the prayer watches to your advantage so as to effectively wage persistent and intense warfare in special cases. It has been tried and tested – believe me. It yields tremendous results. When sleep gets sweetest and deepest, that is when the enemy attacks.

Matthew 13:25 - *But while men slept, his enemy came and sowed tares among the wheat and went his way.*

Prayer is the labor room of champions – the place where great destinies are born. Brethren, you need to pray tirelessly. Prayer delivers what God conceives. When God shows you His will through a vision or a word of prophecy, you must pray it into manifestation. Paul speaking to Timothy in 1 Timothy 1:18 said,

This charge I commit to you, son Timothy, according to the prophecies previously made concerning you, that by them you may wage the good warfare.

Daniel prayed and he became great, succeeding four kings. Esther prayed and she became great (she became the first lady). Hannah prayed in 1 Samuel and gave birth to one of Israel's greatest prophets. Anna the widow prayed for over 80 years until she saw the Lord Jesus face-to-face (Luke 2:36-38). Jesus himself fasted and prayed and as a result the whole world is yet to recover from the three years of His earthly ministry. Paul prayed in tongues more than his peers; see the exploits he commanded! Prayer brings the will of God to pass. Prophecies are brought to manifestation through prayers. Did you know that there is a prayer censer in heaven, collecting the prayers of the saints? (Revelation 8:3-5).

Also in a book called Outliers[1], the 10,000-Hour Rule was shown as a secret key to success – the author said that *whatever you do for 10,000 hours, you become a genius at it.*" He gave a lot of earthly examples but I dare say that the day that you put in your 10,000 hours in prayer, things will begin to happen for you. I'm talking about observing the prayer watches 8 times a day, personal and corporate fasting and prayer, interceding for your nation and generation – not selfish "Gimme, Gimme, my name is Jimmy" prayers.

Let us take a quick look at Jacob's encounter with the Lord in the place of prayer. He travailed in prayer and got another chance to revisit destiny with a brand new name.

> **Genesis 32:24,26,28** - *Then Jacob was left alone; and a Man wrestled with him until the breaking of day. And He said, "Let Me go, for the day breaks."But he said, "I will not let You go unless You bless me!" And He said, "Your name shall no longer be called Jacob, but Israel; for you have struggled with God and with men, and have prevailed."*

What is that looming problem that will not let you dare go back home? What is that perpetual affliction or household trend or that family demon or wicked personality? Who is that unrepentant adversary or evil pursuer? What is that constant reminder of shame and defeat from your past? It is time to bring it before the altar of the Lord. It is time to PUSH! It is time to travail. It is time to Pray Until Something Happens! Like Jacob, you must do it alone before the Lord; you must put the wood in order like Elijah (your strong reasons from His Word). You must observe the prayer watches with fasting and prayer (the midnight and the 3 a.m.

---

[1] Gladwell, M. (2008). Outliers: The story of success. New York: Little, Brown.

watch are great for this type of warfare). You must cry out to God at your meeting place – the altar. You must sound the alarm of praise! You must fill up the golden censer in heaven! You will emerge from this fast a champion in Jesus' name.

DAY 15 PRAYER POINTS:

1. Thank You Lord for the gift of salvation through the blood of Jesus Christ that allows me to come boldly to the throne of grace that I may obtain mercy and find grace to help in time of need.

2. Thank You Lord for the restoration of lost opportunities and lost blessings that I begin to enjoy as the year turns into a new one. Thank You Lord for crowning this year with goodness and your paths dropping fatness for me.

3. Thank You Lord for the grace I enjoy in You for tangible and intangible blessings. Thank You Lord for the blessings of family, health, safety and provision on a daily basis.

4. Thank You Lord for the revelation knowledge you are imparting to me during this fasting and praying season. Thank You Lord for the provision of the flesh and blood of Jesus in the communion table.

5. Father Lord, as I praise You, visit all my stubborn pursuers in Jesus' name. Contend with every contender and deliver me from every strange battle from my father's house, my mother's house. Deliver me from all the battles inherited through marriage.

6. I receive a fresh fire to pray passionately like Elijah. Baptize me with the spirit of grace and supplication so that I can persevere in the labor room of prayer. Grant me the power to pray through to breakthrough.

7. From today, I wage a good warfare with every word of prophecy spoken into my life. I refute every negative pronouncement and silence every evil tongue that rises against me. No weapon fashioned against me shall prosper and every diviner working against my household will turn mad.

> **Isaiah 44:25** - *Who frustrates the signs of the babblers, And drives diviners mad; Who turns wise men backward, And makes their knowledge foolishness.*

8. Like Jacob, as I bow to my God in prayer and praise, my enemies begin to bow before me. As I pray without ceasing, mountains are overturned from their roots and crooked paths are made straight before me. I become a terror to the kingdom of darkness.

9. Father Lord, I operate with the same anointing as my Lord Jesus Christ in prayer and fasting. The seas and the winds obey me and my prayer of faith heals the sick. I will walk in the fullness of The Great Commission and demons will tremble out of their hiding places at my command in Jesus' name.

10. I receive double unction to intercede for my nation and generation. I know of things before they happen. My household and I are first partakers of divine blessings. We are blessed to be blessings to our world and the impact we make transcends our generation in Jesus' name.

11. Father Lord, use me to display your glory. Move me from the valley to the mountaintop. Show the world that You are the same yesterday, today and forever more. You lifted Esther; You blessed Abraham and gave Jacob a new life and a new name. Do this for me before this year is over.

12. Champions are born in the labor room of prayer and great destinies are birthed in the delivery room of prayer. Make me a spiritual midwife raising an army of intercessors and kingdom champions that will storm the world for You.

Give thanks for answered prayers!

DAY 16
TOUCH NOT MY ANOINTED

Today is the sixteenth day of the 21 days of The Chosen Fast. Uzziah was sixteen years old when he became king, and as long as he sought the Lord, God made him prosper (2 Chronicles 26:3-5). I declare that the Lord will make you to prosper as you continue to seek Him in these 21 days of fasting and prayer.

Today, we will be looking at some wicked kings in the Bible and how God rebuked them on behalf of His children. Who were these wicked kings? And what do they stand for? We see some of them in Psalm 136:15,17-20,

> *But overthrew Pharaoh and his army in the Red Sea, For His mercy endures forever; To Him who struck down great kings, For His mercy endures forever; And slew famous kings, For His mercy endures forever—Sihon king of the Amorites, For His mercy endures forever; And Og king of Bashan, For His mercy endures forever—this God loves you dearly and will slay kings because of His enduring mercies for you.*

These kings are also known as princes in the Bible (the word *principality* is derived from the word *prince*).

Ephesians 6:12 - *For we do not wrestle against flesh and blood, but against principalities, against powers, against the rulers of the darkness of this age, against spiritual hosts of wickedness in the heavenly places.*

Behind every affliction is a ruling prince or principality.

The first king or principality we will look at is Pharaoh. Pharaoh is the title of a prince of darkness that afflicts God's chosen people. It is that evil power that will go to any extent to limit the work of your hands and is usually threatened by your destiny and progress. It is the force that exchanges your work and blessing for profitless hard labor and toiling.

Exodus 1:11,14 - *Therefore they set taskmasters over them to afflict them with their burdens. And they built for Pharaoh supply cities, Pithom and Raamses. And they made their lives bitter with hard bondage—in mortar, in brick, and in all manner of service in the field. All their service in which they made them serve was with rigor.*

Is there a trend of generational poverty or failure in your family? Are people not able to get past a certain level of success in your immediate or extended family? Is there a case of chronic debt or borrowing in your life, working tirelessly but having nothing to show for it? You may need to address the forces of Egypt today!

The second king we will look at is Herod. Who is Herod? Herod is the title of a bloodthirsty principality seeking for the head of God's chosen in life and ministry. There was one Herod in Matthew 2 who wanted the head of Jesus and he killed all the children aged 3 years and below. There was another Herod in Mark 6 who beheaded John the Baptist and a third Herod in Acts 12 who beheaded James and wanted the head of Peter the Apostle. This wicked force usually cuts short the life of God's elect, because he feels threatened by them. He is afraid of the anointing and calling upon their lives. He wants to stop the exploits they are making for the kingdom and cannot stand the fact that they are setting people free or actualizing their God-given destinies. The operation of this wicked prince must be stopped in your life today in Jesus' name!

The next king or principality we will look at is Sennacherib. This is a wicked king who threatens complete take over and utter destruction for God's elect. See how his army was defeated and he died like a rat in Isaiah 37:36-38,

> *Then the angel of the Lord went out, and killed in the camp of the Assyrians one hundred and eighty-five thousand; and when people arose early in the morning, there were the corpses—all dead. So Sennacherib king of Assyria departed and went away, returned home, and remained at Nineveh. Now it came to pass, as he was worshiping in the house of Nisroch his god, that his sons Adrammelech and Sharezer struck him down with the sword; and they escaped into the land of Ararat. Then Esarhaddon his son reigned in his place.*

Is there any threat against your life right now? Call on the Lord of hosts, the mighty Man of war, to take over on your behalf.

Another principality or king that fought against God's people is Balak, king of Moabites. He will stop at nothing to pay for divinations and enchantments to work against God's children.

This evil personality is ready to use any form of dark magic against you. See Numbers 22:2&7,

> *Now Balak the son of Zippor saw all that Israel had done to the Amorites. So the elders of Moab and the elders of Midian departed with the diviner's fee in their hand, and they came to Balaam and spoke to him the words of Balak.*

This principality is very crafty looking for your moment of weakness to strike. When he couldn't get the children of Israel through divinations and enchantment, he resorted to trapping them with their sin. The hired Diviner declared in Numbers 23:23 that they were un-cursable and untouchable! This was so until they messed up in Numbers 25:1-2.

Another principality is Sisera. This is the principality that fights against the star of God's anointed. Your star is your essence, your glory or virtue – the strength or quality of your rising! See Judges 4 & 5.

There are other evil kings like Abimelech who attacks the marriage of God's chosen and fights over their inheritance (Genesis 20,21,26); Goliath the power that defies the army of God; Haman the Agagite who contends against God's people especially in his office or positions of authority; kings Og and Sihon who just want to resist doors. Still, there are wicked forces like Jezebel, Delilah and Herodias. Their mission is the same - to behead, destroy and subvert destinies.

Finally, there is one who resists the prayer of the saints.

Daniel 10:12-13 - *Then he said to me, "Do not fear, Daniel, for from the first day that you set your heart to understand, and to* *humble yourself before your God, your words were heard; and I have come because of your words. But the prince of the kingdom of Persia withstood me twenty-one days; and behold, Michael, one of the chief princes, came to help me, for I had been left alone there with the kings of Persia.*

He is a wicked force that is still resisting God's people today, if you let him. Have you been praying about a matter for a long time and there seems to be no result? An evil prince might be involved.

We will call on Jesus Christ the Anointed One and His Anointing that breaks every yoke. The Bible says that He is the Light that shines in darkness and darkness cannot comprehend Him (John 1:5). We are going to break that wicked chain of failed achievements and destroy every yoke of barrenness with the power in the blood of Jesus. The Bible says that He prepares a table before me in the presence of my enemies and anoints my head with oil my cup runs over (Psalm 23:5). This signifies the communion table proclaiming the victory won by His death on the cross and the anointing oil with the inherent power in it that breaks every yoke.

Isaiah 10:27 - *It shall come to pass in that day that his burden will be taken away from your shoulder, And his yoke from your neck, And the yoke will be destroyed because of the anointing oil.*

The blood of Jesus silences every contention and disgraces principalities and powers (Colossians 2:15). Today, the powers that make a man to keep working like an elephant but continue eating like an ant will be slaughtered on this altar of the Lord by the power in the blood of Jesus.

DAY 16 PRAYER POINTS:

1. Thank You Lord Jesus for the overcoming faith that You bestowed to me; the victory that overcomes the wicked one. Thank You Lord for making me more than a conqueror through Your blood.

2. Thank You Lord Father for fighting all my battles as the Man of War; thank You for defeating every enemy in my bloodline and my ancestry.

3. Thank You Lord Holy Spirit for the revelation knowledge I enjoy from You and thank You for teaching my fingers to fight and my hands to war.

4. Thank You Lord for writing my name in the Lamb's Book of life and for the everlasting victory of salvation and redemption from sin.

5. Father Lord, go ahead of me to fight all my battles before they manifest in the physical. I plead the blood of Jesus over every strange battle arrayed against my household.

6. Mighty Man in battle, destroy every force of Egypt limiting the work of my hands and attacking my staff of bread. By reason of this chosen fast, I break every yoke of poverty and hardship in Jesus' name.

7. From today, I operate under the covenant of multiplication and increase in Christ Jesus in every area of my life, work and ministry. I will no longer sweat, toil or struggle because Jesus paid the price.

8. I break every force of regression and circle movements in my journey; I arrive at my destination quicker and fulfill God's mandate for every season, according to divine timing. I recover my time and blessing from wasters and emptiers in Jesus' name.

9. Father Lord, baptize my prayer life with fresh fire so that I can blaze through the dark places of the earth, setting captives free from the hold of the enemy and letting the oppressed go free for your glory.

10. Heavenly Father, I receive fresh oil to break the yoke of sickness, barrenness, poverty and non-achievement in my location, nation and generation. No evil force can touch me and no divination can work against me in Jesus' name.

11. Captain of the hosts, I invite you from the communion table and I declare that the anointing breaks the yoke in this situation (mention it before the Lord). Anoint something as a point of contact; for healing, touch the area; for marriage, anoint your home; for finances, use your check book; for jobs, use your diploma etc.

12. Now enforce the Word of God over specific areas you are experiencing a challenge. Enforce your authority now!

Speak!!

Pharaoh, take your hands off my work and finances in Jesus' name.
I silence every force of Haman in my career and promotion.
You spirit of Egypt, give me back my children and my increase.

You evil prince of Persia resisting any prayers, be roasted up by fire.

Spirit of iniquity operating in my neighborhood, the blood of Jesus is against you.

You prince of violence my area, I unseat you and cast you out in Jesus' mighty name.

I break every yoke of barrenness that runs in families in Jesus' name.

I break free from every chain of non-achievement.

I begin to work like an ant and eat like an elephant.

Every spirit slowing people down, catch fire.

Every power that resists my rising star, be shattered to pieces.

You molester of destinies called Herod, the Lord rebuke you.

I am the Lord's anointed and so you cannot touch me or anyone associated with me.

You evil pursuer, be swallowed up in the red sea of the blood.

You night marauder the angels of the Lord pursue you and strike you.

Give thanks for answered prayers!

DAY 17
WEAPONS OF WAR

Today is the seventeenth day of The Chosen Fast. What is the relevance of the number 17? The number 17 reveals the difference between the Old and the New Covenant. The Old Covenant speaks of anger, fire, tempest, scattering, and death! The New Covenant speaks of mercy, gathering, reconciliation and life! While the old is a shadow of the new, the New Testament is the unveiling of the old.

The tone of warfare is evident in Hebrews 12:18-24, where the distinction between the old and new covenants are made. The whole Bible is filled with different stories about warfare. The Bible started in Genesis with a battle and ended in Revelation with a battle. And in Luke 10:19, Jesus gave us power and authority. For what? To do warfare! Our God is a Man of War, Jehovah is His name! Life is a war. Two forces are involved – the Lord God and His hosts against the devil and his fallen angels/demons. This battle is not in the physical realm but in the spirit realm.

2 Corinthians 10:3-5 - *For though we walk in the flesh, we do not war according to the flesh. For the weapons of our warfare are not carnal but mighty in God for pulling down strongholds, casting down arguments and every high thing that exalts itself against the* *knowledge of God, bringing every thought into captivity to the obedience of Christ.*

There are weapons needed to engage in this war. Our Father is a warrior and so are we. Whether you like it or not – accept Christ or not – you will experience, encounter or engage in a spiritual battle at one time or the other in your life. You cannot escape warfare; it is part of life.

When men go to war, they bring back captives and spoils of war. The enemy has taken many prisoners from this war and our Lord Jesus Christ came just to break them out of satan's jail. He broke Paul and Silas out of prison with praise (Acts 16) and He broke Peter out with prayer (Acts 12). He is the Commander of the armies of Israel. He is the Master Jail Breaker; He came to set the captives free from bloodthirsty demons!

> **Isaiah 49:24-26** - *Shall the prey be taken from the mighty, or the captives of the righteous be delivered? But thus says the Lord:"Even the captives of the mighty shall be taken away, And the prey of the terrible be delivered; For I will contend with him who contends with you,And I will save your children. I will feed those who oppress you with their own flesh, And they shall be drunk with their own blood as with sweet wine. All flesh shall know that I, the Lord, am your Savior, and your Redeemer, the Mighty One of Jacob."*

God will stop at nothing to defend His own. He used natural disaster to defeat Pharaoh in the book of Exodus, even animals were enlisted in this warfare (flies, locust, frogs and lice). The forces of nature took part in this warfare (hail, darkness, disease, boils, death and the water refused to cooperate with the enemy in Egypt). God used the wind to fight for His own and covered them with pillars of cloud and fire. He drowned the army of Pharaoh in the Red Sea. He has killed many enemies in their sleep and still allows them to fall under evil slumber. He has used the angel of death to kill and will not hesitate to use it again. He has wiped off a nation with his own nuclear weapon (rain from heaven); He has sunk great walls of obstruction to make way for His children to pass through. He has used fear, terror and confusion before and specializes in using earthquakes with lightening and thunder.

He can use His chariots of fire or blazing swords of fire like the one guarding the Garden of Eden. He can stop the sun and moon to make a point and He will not hesitate to use madness on anyone who is using divinations and enchantment against His elect. He can even employ the forces of evil to help destroy one another according to Proverbs 16:4,

> *The Lord hath made all things for himself: yea, even the wicked for the day of evil. He is the Lord of Host: all host both good and bad.*

They all submit to Him. Hand over your battles to Him - stop struggling on your own, He is more than enough! Today, the Red Sea that drowns your enemy is the blood of Jesus! The Bible makes us to understand that the blood of Jesus and the word of our testimony are more than enough.

Revelation 12:11 - *And they overcame him by the blood of the Lamb and by the word of their testimony, and they did not love their lives to the death.*

How do we overcome by the words of our testimony? By

proclaiming the finished work of Christ through His death on the Cross of Calvary over every negative situation. And His name brings the greatest foe to his knees – no matter his position or title!

> **Philippians 2:9-11** - *Therefore God also has highly exalted Him and given Him the name which is above every name, that at the name of Jesus every knee should bow, of those in heaven, and of those on earth, and of those under the earth, and that every tongue should confess that Jesus Christ is Lord, to the glory of God the Father.*

The New Testament reveals how to combine the 7 weapons of our warfare in Ephesians 6:10-18. The weapons listed are:

There are seven listed:
1. Helmet of salvation
2. Breastplate of righteousness
3. Belt of truth
4. Shoe of preparation of the gospel
5. Shield of faith
6. Sword of the spirit
7. Prayer and supplication in the spirit

Prayer is the all-time ballistic weapon of mass destruction, and embedded in prayer is praise! You are not the one fighting the war to win. Jesus already won; you only need to key into His finished work using the weapons above.

DAY 17 PRAYER POINTS:

1. Thank You Heavenly Father because in Christ Jesus I have overcome the wicked one and greater is He that is in me than he that is in the world. Thank You Lord for translating me from darkness into Your marvelous light.

2. Thank You Lord for winning impossible battles for me and for delivering my household from seen and unseen battles throughout the year. Thank You Lord for stepping ahead of me to finish every unfinished battle.

3. Thank You Lord for the perfect peace of mind that comes from knowing that You have defeated the enemy of my faith. Thank You Lord for the Name, Blood and Your Word in the person of Jesus Christ.

4. Thank You Lord for the assurance of faith I have in You with the revelation knowledge from This Chosen Fast. Every trend of household wickedness and oppression is destroyed and we are free from every burden in Jesus' name!

5. Father Lord, I enforce the finished work of Christ on the issue of my ...(*mention it before the Lord e.g. marriage, career, health, ministry, fruitfulness*). I break free from every yoke. I am free! I am empowered to fulfill destiny!

6. Captain of the hosts, I release every stubborn pursuer to Your hands and turn over every strange battle to You. As I praise You, let every evil personality gathering against me experience all the plagues of Egypt and if they do not repent, bury them alive with your earthquake.

7. Poverty, this is where we part ways; heavy burdens of debt, it is time for you to go! Sickness, you cannot function in my life. Condemnation and guilt, your time is up! Failure, your tenure is over! Stagnation, I have an appointment with speedy progress and you spirit of death, my Master is Christ!

8. As I engage in prayer and praise warfare, my knowledge in Christ increases and I am able to teach others also. As I intercede for the land, I begin to see light shine in my location, nation and generation.

9. As a good soldier of Jesus Christ, I grow in strength by the Spirit in my inner man. I manifest the fruits of the Spirit (such as love, patience and endurance). I please my Maker in all things.

10. I win every mind battle that the enemy throws at me. My weapons of warfare are not carnal but mighty in God for pulling down strongholds, casting down arguments and every high thing that exalts itself against the knowledge of God, bringing every thought into captivity to the obedience of Christ.

11. As I break bread daily, I proclaim the Lord's death till He comes. I lay claim to my perfected health. I access my increase and prosperity in Christ Jesus. I lay hold on eternal life and flourish in every area of my life for God's glory.

12. No weapon fashioned against me shall prosper, every tongue of divination is disgraced. I plead the blood of Jesus over my family. I break down any evil altar operating in the physical or spiritual realm against me. I stand on the finished work of Christ.

Give thanks for answered prayers!

DAY 18
PRAYER EVANGELISM

Today is the eighteenth day of The Chosen Fast. Today, every bond of wickedness is broken in Jesus' name! According to Luke 13:11-13, there was a woman who had a spirit of infirmity for eighteen years, and was bent over and could in no way raise herself up. But when Jesus saw her, He called her to Him and said to her, "Woman, you are loosed from your infirmity." And He laid His hands on her, and immediately she was made straight, and glorified God. No matter how long that affliction has been going, this 18th day of the fast is the expiration date. You are going from this altar free, to fulfill your calling and victorious destiny in the mighty name of Jesus.

The topic of discussion today is concerning the Ministry of Reconciliation. What does reconciliation mean? It means to restore to agreement or harmony; to settle a dispute or win over to friendship. Why do we need reconciliation if all is well? When God made man in Genesis 1, He came daily to fellowship with him in the cool of the day. But that was abruptly stopped when the serpent showed up in Genesis 3. Sin came into the picture, severing the cord between God and man. Ever since that incident in the Garden of Eden, the mission of the Godhead has been to restore that broken fellowship between God and man. The second Adam (Jesus Christ) started that journey in another garden called Gethsemane, where He prayed. He died for us and shed His blood as the final price for sin. We have been reconciled to God through Christ and we are also called into the same assignment to reconcile or win over the world to the Lord. We are called to share the Good News that God loves them and that He is not mad at them; rather, He is mad about them.

The ministry of Reconciliation is God's idea. God has called you and I to join Him in this glorious mission to bear fruits, in John 15:16 Jesus said,

> *You did not choose Me, but I chose you and appointed you that you should go and bear fruit, and that your fruit should remain, that whatever you ask the Father in My name He may give you.*

Hallelujah! Within that scripture is the key to answered prayers. When you bear fruits that remain, you will have an open access in prayer – anything you ask will be done. God is very passionate about winning souls; the entire Bible is written about this. If you run with the Father's highest priority, then you will get all your priorities met as well. He will ensure that you will receive all your desires and this is confirmed in Psalm 37:4,

> *Delight yourself also in the Lord, And He shall give you the desires of your heart.*

Have you heard of a concept called PRAYER-EVANGELISM? It is winning souls through fervent and consistent prayers. Psalm 2:8 says,

> *Ask of Me, and I will give You the nations for Your inheritance,*

And the ends of the earth for Your possession.

If you are too timid to preach, at least you can pray! Nothing happens by accident. God planted you into that neighborhood because He needs you to intercede for the people and take over the land for Him. Stop waiting for someone else to do it; that is your mission from Him. You are the change agent that city has been waiting for all these years.

Daniel was placed in the palaces of different kings to convert them to God. He eventually touched Nebuchadnezzar and Cyrus. Cyrus was referred to as God's anointed in Isaiah 45:1-3. He was ordained by God to release the people of God from the bondage in Babylon. So also was Esther and Mordecai – they were planted in the land to effect change in the constitution for God and His people. Paul was a scholar so he could engage the philosophers and intellectuals of his time in discussions about the Lord. He was a witness for Christ before many kings and governors.

You may be the only true Christian that will work in that organization; don't ever forget the real reason why you are there! You are there not to blend in but to stand out for Him. You are the epistle that men read (2 Corinthians 3:2). That profession was not a mistake, it was actually God's idea and what He had in mind was reconciliation – salvation for all men in all spheres of life.

Do you have a prayer list for your unsaved friends, neighbors, bosses or co-workers? They already know there is something different about you. Depending on your level of walk with the Lord, you may still be too timid to share the Gospel with them but you can pray. You can intercede for them. In fact, your prayer has tremendous power because you will be able to disarm any strong man controlling their lives. There is a controlling force that influences everyone who is not yet saved. We were all once under that influence before we became born-again (Ephesians 2:2). That is why, regardless of how many times they are preached to, people find it difficult to yield.

> **2 Corinthians 4:4** - *Whose minds the god of this age has blinded, who do not believe, lest the light of the gospel of the glory of Christ, who is the image of God, should shine on them.*

Paul was committed to winning souls and he told his spiritual son, Timothy, to do the work of an evangelist.

> **2 Timothy 4:5** - *But you be watchful in all things, endure afflictions, do the work of an evangelist, fulfill your ministry.*

Are you fulfilling your ministry of reconciliation? If not, don't feel condemned! You can start now in the place of prayer, actively interceding for souls. Start compiling your list today.

I remember when I was in college years ago, I interceded for several classmates and roommates; today, they are on fire for the Lord. I also had a rich relative to whom I was too timid to share the gospel with, but I kept praying, writing letters and sending spiritual materials; eventually, the individual accepted Christ on the deathbed. In one of the letters, I wrote about the parable of the rich fool, asking "What will it profit a man to gain the whole world but lose his own soul?" This resulted in an open rebuke from this person to me, but I did not stop. I look forward to seeing this loved one on resurrection morning!

You also need to know God's Word and grow in it. How can you share the Good News if you are not familiar with it yourself?

2 Timothy 2:15 - *Be diligent to present yourself approved to God, a worker who does not need to be ashamed, rightly dividing the word of truth.*

Read books about evangelism and soul winning. You are the light of the world and the salt of the earth. Let your light shine! Stop being so timid; you are the solution the whole world is crying for! Go ye and preach the good news – God's love letter to His entire creation – baptizing and making disciples in Jesus' name. Go out; make friends for Him. Reconcile man to God; tell them He is mad about them and not mad at them! Take a prayer walk around your neighborhood, praying in tongues. Take over the land for Him, like the children of Israel walked round Jericho. You will then decree a thing and it will be established unto you! That is the key to answered prayers!!

DAY 18 PRAYER POINTS:

1. Thank You Father for qualifying me to be a partaker of the inheritance of the saints in Christ Jesus. Thank You Lord for delivering me from the power of darkness and translating me into the Kingdom of Your marvelous light.

2. Thank You Lord for the redemption through the blood of Jesus and the complete forgiveness of my sins. Thank You Lord for counting me worthy to be called Your ambassador.

3. Thank You Lord for opening the eyes of my understanding to know the hope of this calling and the riches of the inheritance I have in You. I am grateful for the spirit of wisdom and revelation in the knowledge of You!

4. Father, I bow my knees in reverence of You for strengthening me with might through Your spirit in the inner man. Thank You Lord for establishing me in the faith and causing me to be grounded and rooted in Your love that passes all knowledge.

5. Heavenly Father I pray that utterance may be given to me, that I may open my mouth boldly to make known the mystery of the gospel, for which I am an ambassador, that I may speak as I ought to speak to people I meet at school, work or my neighborhood.

6. I pray that I abound more in knowledge and discernment so that I manifest excellence in word and in deeds. I pray that my light will shine so that many will be reconciled to God through my life and testimony.

7. I receive the grace to labor fervently in the place of prayer and the Word so that I can stand perfect and complete in the will of God for my life. I pray that I will be unwearied and steadfast in my prayer life interceding for my loved ones.

8. I pray that the Word of the Lord will spread rapidly from my local church and ministry into our community, running its course such that the knowledge of the Lord will cover the earth as the sand covers the sea shore, all across the globe.

9. I pray for all my spiritual children (*mention them by name*) that Christ be formed in them and they will walk, live and conduct themselves in a manner worthy of the Lord, fully pleasing to Him in all things, bearing fruit in every good work and steadily growing and increasing in the knowledge of God with fuller, deeper, and clearer insight in Jesus' name.

10. From today, I bear fruits as an ambassador and a minister of reconciliation in Jesus' name. I live according to the mandate of bearing fruits that abide and my prayer life becomes a joy and not a chore.

11. As I delight myself in the Lord all my heart desires are met. As I decree a thing, it is established unto me. I increase in strength and exploits and I am empowered for signs and wonders! I witness to the lost and deliver the oppressed in my location, nation and generation in Jesus' name.

12. Now ask, seek, knock! Mention that area of need before the Lord. You have a blank check according to Matthew 7:7-8, *"Ask, and it will be given to you; seek, and you will find; knock, and it will be opened to you. For everyone who asks receives, and he who seeks finds, and to him who knocks it will be opened."*

Give thanks for answered prayers!

SOME PAULINE PRAYERS *(adapted from the writings of Apostle Paul)*

Ephesians 3:14-19 - *For this reason I bow my knees to the Father of our Lord Jesus Christ, from whom the whole family in heaven and earth is named, that He would grant you, according to the riches of His glory, to be strengthened with might through His Spirit in the inner man, that Christ may dwell in your hearts through faith; that you, being rooted and grounded in love, may be able to comprehend with all the saints what is the width and length and depth and height— to know the love of Christ which passes knowledge; that you may be filled with all the fullness of God.*

Colossians 1:9-11 - *For this reason we also, since the day we heard it, do not cease to pray for you, and to ask that you may be filled with the knowledge of His will in all wisdom and spiritual understanding; that you may walk worthy of the Lord, fully pleasing Him, being fruitful in every good work and increasing in the knowledge of God; strengthened with all might, according to His glorious power, for all patience and longsuffering with joy;*

Colossians 1:12-14 - *Giving thanks to the Father who has qualified us to be partakers of the inheritance of the saints in the light. He has delivered us from the power of darkness and conveyed us into the kingdom* *of the Son of His love, in whom we have redemption through His blood, the forgiveness of sins.*

2 Thessalonians 1:11-12 - *Therefore we also pray always for you that our God would count you worthy of this calling, and fulfill all the good pleasure of His goodness and the work of faith with power, that the name of our Lord Jesus Christ may be glorified in you, and you in Him, according to the grace of our God and the Lord Jesus Christ.*

Colossians 1:9-12 (AMP) - *For this reason we also, from the day we heard of it, have not ceased to pray and make special request for you, asking that you may be filled with the full deep and clear knowledge of His will in all spiritual wisdom in comprehensive insight into the ways and purposes of God and in understanding and discernment of spiritual things— That you may walk live and conduct yourselves in a manner worthy of the Lord, fully pleasing to Him and desiring to please Him in all things, bearing fruit in every good work and steadily growing and increasing in and by the knowledge of God with fuller, deeper, and clearer insight, acquaintance, and recognition. We pray that you may be invigorated and strengthened with all power according to the might of His glory, to exercise every kind of endurance and patience perseverance and forbearance with joy, Giving thanks to the Father, Who has qualified and made us fit to share the portion which is the inheritance of the saints God's holy people in the Light.*

Philemon 1:4-6 - *I thank my God, making mention of you always in my prayers, hearing of your love and faith which you have toward the Lord Jesus and toward all the saints, that the sharing of your faith may become effective by the acknowledgment of every good thing which is in you in Christ Jesus.*

Ephesians 1:17-19 - *That the God of our Lord Jesus Christ, the Father of glory, may give to you the spirit of wisdom and revelation in the knowledge of Him, the eyes of your understanding being enlightened; that you may know what is the hope of His calling, what are the riches of the glory of His inheritance in the saints, and what is the exceeding greatness of His power toward us who believe, according to the working of His mighty power.*

DAY 19
THE VOICE OF THE LORD

Today is the nineteenth day of The Chosen Fast. Today, we are looking at the topic called The Voice of the Lord! When He utters His words, He never turns back from it.

Numbers 23:19 - *God is not a man, that He should lie, Nor a son of man, that He should repent. Has He said, and will He not do? Or has He spoken, and will He not make it good?*

Titus 1:2 also says God cannot lie! See Hebrews 6:18,

That by two immutable things, in which it is impossible for God to lie, we might have strong consolation, who have fled for refuge to lay hold of the hope set before us.

The voice of the Lord is mighty and full of majesty! His voice thunders, burns and breaks just to bring you peace. Let us look at Psalm 29 together:

Psalm 29:1-11 - *Give unto the Lord, O you mighty ones, Give unto the Lord glory and strength. Give unto the Lord the glory due to His name; Worship the Lord in the beauty of holiness. The voice of the Lord is over the waters; The God of glory thunders; The Lord is over many waters. The voice of the Lord* *is powerful;The voice of the Lord is full of majesty. The voice of the Lord breaks the cedars,Yes, the Lord splinters the cedars of Lebanon. He makes them also skip like a calf,Lebanon and Sirion like a young wild ox. The voice of the Lord divides the flames of fire. The voice of the Lord shakes the wilderness;The Lord shakes the Wilderness of Kadesh. The voice of the Lord makes the deer give birth,And strips the forests bare; And in His temple everyone says, "Glory!" The Lord sat enthroned at the Flood, And the Lord sits as King forever. The Lord will give strength to His people; The Lord will bless His people with peace.*

The voice of the Lord is so powerful that it slices to pieces the biggest and tallest tree in the forest without any effort. The voice will help a laboring deer give birth without epidural. The voice of the Lord thunders and burns like fire.

There were several patriarchs who heard the audible voice of the Lord. Moses heard the voice of the Lord. Till Moses died, he served as God's oracle. Samuel heard the voice of the Lord and was also God's spokesperson till he finished his assignment on earth. Elijah heard the still small voice of the Lord and his voice was feared throughout the lands. Saul of Tarsus heard the voice of our Lord and he became transformed into Paul the apostle of New Testament mysteries (even after his death, his voice is still heard). Jesus our Messiah was openly acknowledged and approved by the voice of the Father and the world is yet to recover from that encounter.

When you hear the voice of the Lord, it empowers you to be a voice to your own generation. When you hear the voice of the Lord, you can speak to any dead situation and it will come alive (see Ezekiel 37:3-10). When the voice of the Lord enters into a man, it will turn an ordinary jar of clay to a forceful powerhouse. Remember that the bones of Elisha still carried that residue power that raised a man from the dead (2 Kings 13:21). When you become this power center, forces of darkness bow before you and sickness and germs dry up on contact with you. Airborne diseases become afraid of your household. Hallelujah!

When God's voice openly approves you, the devil will test you. Have you noticed that when a word of prophecy is released concerning you, the enemy fights it so much and makes it look as if that word will never come to pass. That was why Paul told Timothy to wage a good warfare with the words of prophecy released. The devil cannot read God's mind concerning you and neither can he read your mind, but the minute he hears a public proclamation of God's voice concerning you, he attacks that word.

The same was written about our Lord Jesus in Matthew 3:16-17,

> *When He had been baptized, Jesus came up immediately from the water; and behold, the heavens were opened to Him, and He saw the Spirit of God descending like a dove and alighting upon Him. And suddenly a voice came from heaven, saying, "This is My beloved Son, in whom I am well pleased."*

Then in the next chapter,

> **Matthew 4:1** - *Then Jesus was led up by the Spirit into the wilderness to be <u>tempted by the devil.</u>*

The approval of God over your life attracts trials and temptation. Embrace it and rejoice when you see them because without test there is no testimony. Trials always end in triumph, if we hold on to His Word.

> **James 1:2-4** - *My brethren, count it all joy when you fall into various trials, knowing that the testing of your faith produces patience. But let patience have its perfect work, that you may be perfect and complete, lacking nothing.*

Trials perfect you. Stop despising them; trials mature and polish you. They develop your character and make you unshakable and immovable. Just like in school, before every promotion, you get tested; so also in life, the test leads to your testimony.

The voice is only clear to those who have a deep walk with Him – those who hunger and thirst after righteousness; those pant after Him like the deer pants after the water brooks; those who seek Him at the prayer watches; those who hide in the secret place of the most High – studying, meditating, praying and praising. His voice is clear to those who have removed the noise to hear His voice, removing themselves from every distraction to seek Him with all their hearts. Even when Paul was zealous for God in ignorance, he heard His voice but the other men didn't hear what he heard (Acts 9).

A similar thing happened to Daniel (Daniel 10:7), Moses (Exodus 19:16,19) and Jesus (John 12:28-29, Luke 9:32). As Jesus prayed, the appearance of His face was altered, and His robe became white and glistening. He was supernaturally empowered to face His divine assignment as audacious as it was. The multitude came to meet Jesus to heal and deliver them. You life will be transformed and your generation will celebrate God's deposit into your life. You will echo His voice through the uttermost parts of the earth in Jesus' name. Do you know you can hear that voice today, according to Hebrews 1:1-2? By the help of the Holy Spirit you will hear the inaudible and see the invisible from the pages of scriptures (Isaiah 30:21, Psalm 119:18).

DAY 19 PRAYER POINTS:

1. Thank You Father for being the same yesterday, today and forevermore. Thank You Lord for speaking in the past through the prophets and now speaking to us by the Holy Spirit.

2. Thank You Lord for opening my spiritual ears so I can hear the inaudible. Thank You Lord for wakening my ear morning by morning and for giving me the tongue of the learned through redemption in Christ Jesus.

3. Thank You Lord for Your voice that is full of majesty and power! Thank You Lord for the fire from your voice that burns the enemy. The strongest resistance gives way at the sound of Your voice according to Psalm 29.

4. Thank You Lord because when You say a thing, You do it; and when You speak a word, You make it good. I am grateful for all the words You have spoken concerning me and my entire household. I serve a God who cannot lie!

5. Father, from today, let me hear You plainly like Moses. Speak with me face to face. Regardless of the chaos and noise going on around me, cause me to hear Your still small voice like Elijah.

6. From a young age Samuel heard Your voice; let that be the portion of my children and I. Let the words that we speak be backed by heaven and let none fall to the ground when we address situations in our lives, ministry and nation.

7. Heavenly Father, give me a mountain of transfiguration experience like Jesus. Let my life be transformed from one level of glory to another as I look unto Jesus the author and finisher of my faith.

8. Father Lord, because Jesus was tried and tested, let me rejoice when trials come. Help me to rejoice about the testimonies and promotions that are behind the test. As silver is tried seven times in a furnace of fire, let me grow in maturity and character.

9. Father Lord, amplify my voice for Your glory. Let me echo Your power and majesty as I declare Your words to the lost. Let demons come out of all their hideouts, trembling everywhere in Jesus' name. Let me operate by the same anointing, setting captives free and healing the sick.

10. Dear Lord, let Your words in my mouth be a double-edged sword, saving souls and destroying the powers of darkness. Let me operate like my Master who is a Lion and a Lamb, devouring the enemy and healing the broken-hearted. Let me display Your majesty and tenderness with my voice.

11. As I am empowered by Your voice, let my voice go through all the earth preaching the Good News and touching many lives to the uttermost parts of the world for Your glory. Grant me boldness and the strength! Make me fire and water.

12. Look at any situation that has resisted your voice for so long and call down the voice of the Lord on it now! According to Psalm 29, His voice brings fruitfulness, destroys the proud cedar of Lebanon (aka Pharaoh). His voice breaks the strongest resistance. At the sound of His voice demons tremble and sicknesses flee. His voice shakes the unshakable!

Give thanks for answered prayers!

DAY 20
THE RESURRECTION AND THE LIFE

Today is the twentieth day of The Chosen Fast. The number twenty holds a spiritual significance in the Bible for spiritual warfare. In Numbers 1:3, God told Moses to enlist warriors from twenty years old and above—all who are able to go to war in Israel. At 20, you leave childish things and begin to handle matters of adulthood. It is time for you to manifest sonship in the place of prayer. This is explained in Galatians 4:1-7 (you can read it prayerfully for deeper understanding). Congratulations for enlisting as a warrior in the order of the Lord.

Today's topic is The Resurrection and The Life, a title of Jesus Christ. It has to do with what the Bible says in 1 Corinthians 15:26,

The last enemy that will be destroyed is death.

Every dead situation in your life must receive divine attention today in Jesus' name. Whether it is your career, marriage, destiny or health, I declare that The Resurrection and The Life Himself will step into that dead and stinking situation. God has put all things under Christ (1 Corinthians 15:27), who has the keys of hell and death. He took the sting out of death and conquered the grave completely. The Bible makes it clear that those who love Him and have a close walk with Him do not fear death.

> **Revelation 12:11** - *And they overcame him by the blood of the Lamb and by the word of their testimony, and they did not love their lives to the death.*

Many times people quote the first half of this scripture but don't know what to so with the second part. You cannot truly love God or understand the depth of His love for you and be afraid of anything. Perfect love casts out fear – not your own love but His perfect love for you.

Let us take a quick look at those who made nonentity of death through The Resurrection and The Life in the Old and New Testament. Remember The Resurrection and The Life is a person! Moses was a man who had discussions with God on how he will exit the earth. God himself buried him. Jesus said Moses understood The Resurrection and The Life (Luke 20:37-38).

The prophet Elijah went out triumphantly on the chariot of fire cheating death out of his pound of flesh. And in his ministry on the earth raised the dead back to life see1 Kings 17:22. His successor Elisha had double anointing and raised the son of the Shunnamite woman back to life in his lifetime in 2 King 4 but even in his death, his bones raised a dead man back to life as well in 2 Kings 13. Have you also noticed that all these men knew exactly when they will be taken. Moses knew, Elijah knew and Elisha knew. It is time for you to stop fretting and fearing the wrong person.

The one you need to fear is the Resurrection and the Life who has the power to kill and make alive (Matthew 10:28). This God is able to revive dead wombs and resurrect dead situations! Romans 4:19 says that Abraham was not weak in faith, he did not consider his own body, already dead since he was about a hundred years old, and the deadness of Sarah's womb. My question to you is, "What part of your body has the doctor given a dead report about?" The Resurrection and The Life will touch that part of you right now and you shall be made completely whole in Jesus' name!

In Matthew 9, Jesus raised Jairus' daughter back to life saying, "Talitha Cumi." In Acts 9, Peter replicated the same by raising the dead. Peter carried The Resurrection and The Life wherever he went and many miracles were performed such that people brought the sick out into the streets and laid them on beds and couches, that at least the shadow of Peter passing by might fall on some of them. Paul the apostle raised Eutychus from the dead in Acts 20:9-11. All these were termed "unusual miracles" in Acts 19:11-12.

The Bible records in Hebrews 11:35 that women received their dead raised to life again. Like the widow of Nain whose future rested in her dead son but The Resurrection and The life restored her bleak future with color! Today, you can walk with this important personality. He can kill any evil personality on your behalf and make a very important personality out of you. He is the same one who introduced himself as The Resurrection and The Life in John 11:25,

> Jesus said to her, "I am the resurrection and the life. He who believes in Me, though he may die, he shall live.

Jesus just opened His mouth and death gave up Lazarus. When He spoke, every dead cell came alive! When He spoke, all the rottenness left and fresh life came. When he spoke, the maggots and worms that were having a feast on the body of Lazarus gave up what they had eaten. When He uttered His words, every sting of the death and chains of the grave gave way! His words went back in time to restore Lazarus to the state before the sickness came into his body. He can reverse time or fast-forward time!

Are you washed by Jesus' blood and have you made Him your Lord and Savior? If yes, then you need not be afraid anymore because Romans 8:11 says, *"if the Spirit of Him who raised Jesus from the dead dwells in you, He who raised Christ from the dead will also give life to your mortal bodies through His Spirit who dwells in you."* During this time of separation of fasting and prayers, focus intensely on The Resurrection and The Life and death will bow before you. Death is your servant – a vehicle you ride out of this side of eternity to everlasting life, when your assignment on earth is done. Don't be afraid of death anymore. Jesus said in Revelation 1:17-18,

> ... *"Do not be afraid; I am the First and the Last. I am He who lives, and was dead, and behold, I am alive forevermore. Amen. And I have the keys of Hades and of Death.*

He holds that key in our favor. Just be rest assured of His words in Psalm 118:17 that says that you shall not die, but live and declare the works of the Lord. Until your time is done on earth, we will be here together building His Kingdom as we await His return. Even in His wrath, God He said man will live for 120 years (Genesis 6:3). How much more now that His only son has paid the price.

DAY 20 PRAYER POINTS:

1. Thank You Lord Jesus for giving Your life for me so that I can live forevermore. I am grateful to You for giving me the God kind of life that cannot be molested here on earth or in heaven.

2. Thank You Lord ,The Resurrection and The Life, for the key of life and death that You hold in my favor. Thank You Lord for the Passover blood that keeps speaking for me and my entire household.

3. Thank You Lord for the revelation knowledge You have given me from this altar of prayer. Thank You Lord for the entrance of Your Word that brings light and deliverance, according to Psalms 119:130 and Proverbs 11:9b.

4. Thank You Lord for Your hand of protection over me and my family, throughout this year. Thank You Lord for hiding us under the shadow of Your wings through every storm.

5. Resurrection and the Life, show up for me in this matter (mention the area). I need You to revive my marriage, womb, career, business, academics, finances, ministry etc. Let the dry bones live again! Reverse the evil report!

6. Father Lord, let the Blood of Sprinkling and the Passover speak for me in every dark battle. Every evil mercenary sent my way must return to sender in Jesus' name. No evil shall befall me or my household because the law of the Spirit of Life is at work in me.

7. I shall not die but live to declare the glory of the Lord in

the land of the living. I have a blood covenant with Christ Jesus that nullifies any generational covenant or trend of untimely death.

8. From today, nothing is permitted to die around me because greater is He that is in me than he that is in the world. I carry the same Spirit that raised Christ from the dead; my mortal body is quickened for my assignment.

9. Abraham died at a ripe full age of 175; Isaac died at 180. Moses went home at 120; his vision did not grow dim and his natural strength was not abated. I have a better covenant in Christ Jesus so I am satisfied with long life in good health.

10. Like Peter, my shadow heals the sick and like Paul, my apron raises the dead. I manifest my sonship because my Father is The Resurrection and The Life. I will not endure life but enjoy life in abundance.

11. The first Adam was a living soul but the second Adam (Jesus) is a quickening Spirit. My destiny, receive speed; my star, you must arise and shine! I make progress as I fulfill my God-given assignment to humanity.

12. I am empowered as an intercessor to lift up my voice on behalf of the speechless and those appointed to die. I operate as the Lord's battle-ax, destroying the works of death and the destroyer in Jesus' name.

Jeremiah 51:20 - *"You are My battle-ax and weapons of war: For with you I will break the nation in pieces; With you I will destroy kingdoms.*

Give thanks for answered prayers!

DAY 21
A NEW ME

Today is the last day of The Chosen Fast. Congratulations! The twenty-first day represents complete victory as depicted in Daniel 10:3,12-13. Today, that secret petition you have been talking to God about has been granted to you like Daniel in Jesus' name!

The topic for today is A New Me. It is a study that focuses on the character of the eagle. The eagle is a bird of such great character. The eagle is mentioned 39 times in scriptures. The Bible actually encourages us to study the way of the eagle in Proverbs 30:19. The eagle is a great bird that lives by very high standards. It builds its nest in the highest hills or in the stars according to Obadiah 1:4. Unlike other birds, it can walk, run and fly.

The great eagle is a lone ranger, not moving in herds like other birds. It is not afraid to stand alone with God. The eagle is also very selective of the company it keeps. At best, it will fly with other eagles like itself (Proverbs 27:17). Look for friends who will sharpen you, not ones that will quench the Spirit in you by despising you or grumbling or gossiping.

The eagle is a picky eater. No matter how hungry it is, it hunts and eats fresh meat dripping with blood (not dead or stale meat) – this denotes fresh revelation and the blood of Jesus. From today, you will be downloading fresh manna from heaven as you abide in the secret place of the Most High, as you chew on His Word and eat the Communion.

The eagle goes through several changes in the course of its lifetime. As a young eagle, it is taught to fly and hunt for food under very strict training. God wants you to grow; He wants to take you to new heights in your walk with him. Are you ready to walk with Him? Are you ready to pay the price for greatness by leaving your comfort zone? The mother eagle mentors the young – look for people to mentor for the Lord from this day forward.

After about a year, the young eagle is ready to be independent and rolls alone for about 3 years. At age 3, the eagle sheds its black beak for a golden one. That is how you differentiate a young one from an adult. Your mouth must become seasoned with the Word of truth – the sword of the spirit! GET a golden mouth!

> **Luke 21:15** - *For I will give you a mouth and wisdom which all your adversaries will not be able to contradict or resist.*

After this stage, the eagle is ready for mating – the male begins to court the female eagle. She plays real hard to get and won't give in easily. The female eagle tests the male by making him pick her twig, flying really high and dropping real low (sometimes picking up heavy branches). If he can catch it, then she stays with him for the rest of her life. If he fails the test, she moves on to the next eagle that is tenacious enough to meet her standards. The eagle stays committed to one partner for life. If the female dies, the male will stay to raise the eaglets. As a believer you must stay committed. Do not be a Sunday-to-Sunday Christian; you must walk with the Lord daily.

The eagle has great peripheral vision of about 275 degrees and sharp binocular vision 4-8 times stronger than the average human. This speaks of vision and precision. You must be able to see far ahead and deep within (insight). Both are possible by the Holy Spirit. Let no new month or year sneak in on you; several days before the new month/year begins, ask for directions from the Holy Spirit.

The eagle has two enemies – the serpent and the storm. Can you relate to both? When pursued by the enemy, it heads for the sun. It can look directly at the sun because of its unusual eyesight with two different eyelids (there is an inner one that goes across from side to side). Every stubborn pursuer will turn back as you run to the secret place, to the cleft of the rock.

The eagle is very swift, flying at about 100 miles per hour. The eagle does not flap its wings like other birds but actually watches for the current or direction of the wind and uses it to soar; it glides effortlessly on the wind. From today, there will be no more struggles in your life. When men are cast down you will say there is a lifting up! The eagle can spot a storm coming from a great distance and will wait for the right time to ride the storm as it circles higher and higher into the sky. The eagle knows how to follow the leading of the wind and it is not afraid to ride through storms. Other birds get flustered easily but not the eagle. It doesn't cry for food or fret in the storm. It has no fear of adversity. No moaning and complaining or looking for a pity party! It doesn't have a victim's mentality; it has a conqueror's mentality. Our minds need to be transformed to that of a conqueror (Romans 12:2).

The eagle also goes through a process of involuntary change called Molting. It retreats to the mountaintop to shed off its old feathers and renew its youth. The eagle hibernates to rejuvenate for about 40 days, hiding in the cleft of the rock of the highest mountain with no food or water. Jesus fasted for 40 days and Moses also fasted for 40 days – they were both transfigured and transformed by God's glory.

> **Isaiah 40:31** – *But those who wait on the Lord shall renew their strength; They shall mount up with wings like eagles, They shall run and not be weary, They shall walk and not faint.*

The time of renewal is crucial for the eagle's survival, otherwise it will become a prey. Getting rid of old feathers and unnecessary weight allows for swiftness. As a believer, you must also get rid of the weights and sins that easily slow you down (Hebrews 12:1).

Finally, Moses was an eagle who was used to dwelling on the mountaintop. He was transformed by God, such that his face shone and people could not look him in the face. He talked with God face-to-face. He lived to be 120 years with his youth renewed. He was an intercessor and he fasted for forty days many times. He was married to one wife and walked with God all through his life. He went through different phases of change experiencing the first 40 years in Egypt, the next 40 years in the wilderness and then the last 40 years soaring as the leader of God's people. He had the personal testimony of an eagle with God as well as the children of Israel.

The eagle in you must emerge! Enough of walking on the

ground like a chicken! Enough of the flapping of wings, struggling and toiling! No more sweating! It is time to soar!

DAY 21 PRAYER POINTS:

1. Thank You Lord for watching over me as the eagle watches over its young; leading me, instructing me, encircling me and transforming me from one level of glory to another, into the same image as You.

2. Thank You Lord for keeping me as the apple of Your eyes and for Your protection over my entire household. Thank You Lord for satisfying my mouth with good things so that my youth is renewed like the eagle.

3. Thank You Lord for the revelations You have given to me during this 21 days of fasting and prayer. Thank You Lord for showing me the way of the eagle in character, strength and great insight.

4. Lord, I receive the grace to wait upon You constantly from today, maturing and developing my spirit man. I grow in insight and spiritual understanding. I know of things before they happen and operate with a golden mouth according to Luke 21:15.

5. Father Lord, I will soar where others are struggling, operating with the leading and direction of the Holy Spirit. I will take advantage of storms and ride them with mastery in Jesus' name.

6. As I walk through life, I will not faint and as I run the race of destiny, I will not grow weary. I display uncommon physical and spiritual strength; the eagle in me emerges as I take off on a flight, impacting my generation for Jesus.

7. God rides upon the cherubim with the speed of lightning. Because I carry His divine presence, I gain uncommon speed and remain a mystery to the enemy. I become a high flier and defy every law of gravity that keeps people down.

8. Throughout my journey on the earth, my mouth is filled with good things and my youth is renewed like the eagle. My household will not beg for bread, instead our home will be called the house of bread. We will be channels of blessing in Jesus' name.

9. As a great eagle, I raise younger eagles for the Lord. I become a lifetime student of the Word, riding the heights of the earth, eating the produce of the fields, drawing honey from the rock and oil from the flinty rock.

10. My physical and spiritual eyes will not grow dim but my vision will expand. I begin to see and take advantage of uncommon opportunities that produce uncommon wealth. I enjoy the secrets of the Lord in every area of my life.

11. As a new me emerges, I begin to gather with fellow eagles. My life will attract color and my destiny helpers will emerge. My name will be mentioned in kings' palaces and my gifts will make room for me before great men.

12. By reason of the Communion the new me is released! The spirit of the Lord is unveiling the new me and releases the eagle in me. *Speak to the Lord about specific areas of struggle. With the Communion, proclaim the Lord's death over the situation and receive wisdom for exploits.*

Give thanks for answered prayers!

CONCLUSION: A NEW BEGINNING

Fasting and prayer keeps your spirit man strong and it will reflect in your mind and body. To wait on the Lord in fasting means to pray, study the Word and praise the Lord, not just abstaining from food. As you conclude The Chosen Fast, I encourage you to keep on with this spiritual exercise, at least once a week for the rest of your life. It produces tremendous results – as an individual/ministry. There are many testimonies at the back of this book that will encourage you. All of which came out of a season of personal or corporate fast; fasting does not change God's mind about any given situation; it will suppress the flesh so you can clearly hear the voice of the Spirit.

I pray that like the eagle, you will experience the direct ray of the Sun of righteousness. The eagle is the only bird that looks directly at the sun. There is a strong link between the eagle and the sun. Because the eagle builds its nest in the highest mountains, it has the advantage of taking the first look at dawn. There are many pictures depicting the eagle flying in the twilight of the sun at dawn and at its full strength at midday.

As an eagle believer, you have the advantage of taking a peek at the things God has in stock for the rest of your life. God shares His secrets with all those who fear Him and those who seek

Him early. I decree that you will experience a new beginning – a new Dawn – in Christ Jesus. What is the meaning of Dawn? It is the beginning or rising of anything. It means to begin to grow or develop. It also means to begin to be perceived or understood. Those around you will begin to take notice of you for distinction and greatness in Jesus' name. They will notice that you are different and that you carry the light of God.

The dawn is a swift and momentous time to take advantage of. It is a very brief period just before the morning light. It is a time of utmost importance. As an eagle believer, you must be actively engaged in what is called Dawn Patrol (this is a flight mission usually done very early in the morning to detect the enemy's position and survey the environment, like the watchman standing on the tower). It is one of the biggest secrets of the military today. The eagle is known to scout very early in the morning just at the break of dawn. Nothing catches the eagle by surprise. There are matters you have to settle before the day is set and all the evil pronouncements and plan of the enemy is established.

Many world religions take advantage of this early morning watch and use it well to control issues. This was what Joshua and the children of Israel took advantage of in Joshua 6:15-16,

> But it came to pass on the seventh day that they rose early, about the dawning of the day, and marched around the city seven times in the same manner. On that day only they marched around the city seven times. And the seventh time it happened, when the priests blew the trumpets, that Joshua said to the people: "Shout, for the Lord has given you the city!

Some longstanding problems will not give way until you

address them at the morning watch and seize the power of the oppressor or contender of our faith. The psalmist understood the power in this so much that he proclaimed in Psalm 108:2,

Awake, lute and harp! I will awaken the dawn. We must wake up to uncommon worship and praise.

At dawn, we get really comfortable and intensify our sleep. It is very unfortunate that the enemy also takes advantage of this fact, but thanks be to God Almighty for revealing this secret. There is help available at this precious hour. Psalm 46:5 says,

God is in the midst of her, she shall not be moved; God shall help her, just at the break of dawn.

Even Christ defeated death and the grave just at the break of dawn.

Matthew 28:1-4 - *Now after the Sabbath, as the first day of the week began to dawn, Mary Magdalene and the other Mary came to see the tomb. And behold, there was a great earthquake; for an angel of the Lord descended from heaven, and came and rolled back the stone from the door, and sat on it. His countenance was like lightning, and his clothing as white as snow. And the guards shook for fear of him, and became like dead men.*

We have seen how to manifest this light in Isaiah 58:10-12 (The Chosen Fast):

The level of glory God is talking about is for global and generational impact – not anything small or just enough for our bank accounts or to pay our bills. It is beyond what we could ever imagine. I'm sure none of the patriarch's of old knew how many generations after them would still be relishing their testimonies as we are still doing today. That is the dimension God is calling us to, if only we would walk with Him. God is looking for men and women of spiritual substance for generational and global relevance. He said in Matthew 5:13-16,

> *You are the salt of the earth; but if the salt loses its flavor, how shall it be seasoned? It is then good for nothing but to be thrown out and trampled underfoot by men. "You are the light of the world. A city that is set on a hill cannot be hidden. Nor do they light a lamp and put it under a basket, but on a lampstand, and it gives light to all who are in the house. Let your light so shine before men, that they may see your good works and glorify your Father in heaven.*

We need to align ourselves to His mandate and original plan for our lives. There are so many deep secrets He wants to share with you before they become a reality. He is looking for kingdom treasurers to channel His wealth through. He is looking for visionaries like Habakkuk who will maintain a watchtower; or like Daniel who observed the prayer watches. If you want to shine in full strength from today, you must be willing to give up some food, some meat, some of the royal dainties of the king's palace (video games, television programs and social media time etc) and you must be willing to lose some sleep too. I think those make up little prices to pay for incomparable greatness.

> **2 Corinthians 4:17** - *For our light affliction, which is but for a moment, is working for us a far more exceeding and eternal weight of glory.*

Welcome to your new beginning – A new you! A new dawn!

TESTIMONIES

TESTIMONY OF DELIVERANCE

Two weeks ago, you gave me the prayer point for Marital Destiny. So two Sundays ago, I woke up early and prayed those prayers. When I went back to bed, God gave me a dream showing me that I had a spiritual husband attached to me. In the dream, I was lying next to a man and he was forcing me to kiss him and holding my neck and I could not prevent him from doing so. When I woke up, I was shaking but I knew it was because of past sexual sins I committed. I had heard of spiritual husbands but could have never imagined that I could have had one. Well, one of your prayer points said that God should remove any third party involved in my marriage and God showed me that so I could cast it out in prayers.

So I did and prayed. I also asked God to show me where there could be any other cracks in my foundations. All through that week, the enemy attacked me and I started having insomnia and becoming very anxious. God kept on giving me scriptures telling me to be "Strong and courageous" and to keep praying. So I continued.

To cut the long story short, that following Thursday, I was exhausted and I wanted to give up but God lead me to pray one more time (to strike "Syria" until I make an end of it). On Friday morning at 1 a.m., I woke up. God had given me confirmation that I was delivered from the spiritual husband and other spirits. He spoke to me about it but I was still feeling anxious, and I started praising and worshiping God.

Not quite 10 minutes within the worship, I felt a loud and strong wind pass by me. And then, I felt total peace surrounding me (by the east wind, God shattered the ships of Tarshish). "It is done" and "It is finished" were the words God later gave me to confirm the warfare was over.

I truly give God the glory for revelation and deliverance. I would have never known something was wrong with my foundation unless God had showed me. God is truly good and powerful, ALL THE TIME!!!

Thank you Pastor, God used you to start an amazing work of deliverance in me. Thank you for your ministry and for your servitude toward God. I am still praying those prayers points until I meet my mate.

NTPM Member (Illinois USA)

TESTIMONY OF FINANCIAL BREAKTHROUGH

I am an international student earning my masters degree in the United States. I applied offered assistantship that should pay my tuition and fees. Before I came, I was in contact with a professor who assured me a position when I arrived to start school. Unfortunately, I did not get the position and I quickly became financially stranded. A few days before the deadline to my tuition fees (or I would be kicked out of my position and school), I met the coordinator of the Nehemiah Troop Prayer Ministry (NTPM) who advised me to pray and fast for three days and also joined me in the prayer and fasting during those days. To save money, I was then living in the basement of a church with extremely difficult living conditions; I could not even afford to have an apartment.

We started praying for God to reveal Himself in the situation and within a week or two after the fast, I not only got a miracle to pay for school but a lady offered me accommodation for free as long as I teach her my native language. In quick succession, God opened doors for me. I was able to repay my loans, have a car and get a ticket to visit my family without even having to ask for it. I am grateful to God for coming across Nehemiah Troop Prayer Ministry and I encourage you to pray believing God because He still answers prayer.

Student (Illinois-USA)

TESTIMONY OF SPEEDY TURN-AROUND

I am so grateful to God for what He is doing in my life. We have been trying to buy a house, but we were not able to because of our poor credit. I shared with the pastor of Nehemiah Troop and she told me that if God wanted us to buy a house, he would make it possible regardless of how poor the credit score was. So during the 21-day fasting exercise in December, I decided I was going to stand on the promises of God. I even told my sisters and brother to send me their prayer requests.

Two months after the 21 day of prayer and fast, we bought a house!!! And God answered every request that my family sent. To Him be all the glory, power and honor forever and ever. Amen!

Member NTPM - Illinois USA

OTHER VERBAL REPORTS:

1. A family believing God for a favorable ruling in a long-standing and notorious court case joined the 21 days Chosen Fast and experienced favor with the judge after praying in agreement with NTPM prayer lead.

2. Someone who had been jobless and battling bankruptcy joined the prayer and fasting at Nehemiah Troop Prayer Ministry got a miracle job within a few weeks.

3. A student attended the live prayer conference where we shared the word, prayer and the Holy Communion got several job offers within two weeks.

ABOUT RAENI BANKOLE

Raeni Bankole is a minister of the gospel with a three-fold calling to this generation; she was born and raised in Southern Nigeria as Omolaraeni Odewole in a Christian family of 8 children. She relocated to the United States of America in 2001 to further her education.

In 1997, while studying at the University of Ibadan she heard the first call to be used as a "Repairer of the Breach and a Restorer of the path for men to dwell in" according to Isaiah 58:12. She worked passionately in the campus fellowship at the University of Ibadan and later served as one of the pioneering leaders of the Winners Youth Fellowship of the Living Faith Church (Winners Chapel) till she moved to the United States.

In the United States she has served fervently in several ministries under the Redeemed Christian Church of God for over 12 years in the Chicago-land area till she resumed full-time ministry in 2013. She currently runs a vibrant prayer school in the Chicago-land area teaching the word of God and showing the secrets of deliverance by the knowledge of the truth. Her passion is to help individuals birth their God-given vision and to nurture those destinies to complete fulfillment. Many of her teachings can be found on Soundcloud.com @ Nehemiah Troop. She is married to Adebowale Bankole and together they have two lovely children.

Her apostolic calling as a watchman and a voice unto nations operates through different branches of Empowerment

Mission Agency (NPF) a registered non-profit organization in the United States of America with a mission to empower nations through Christ.

Mission: Empowering nations through Christ

Vision: Birthing visions and nurturing destinies.

Repairer of the Breach: She teaches and preaches the word of God bringing many to the saving knowledge of the Lord and restoring many lost destinies to their divine destiny in Christ Jesus. "And they shall build the old waste places: you shall raise up the foundations of many generations; and you shall be called, The repairer of the breach, The restorer of paths to dwell in." (Isaiah 58:12).

A Watchman: As a watchman, she runs an intercessory ministry that has a mandate to raise a global army of intercessors unto the kingdom of our Lord Jesus Christ...I have made you a watchman for the house of Israel; therefore you shall hear a word from My mouth and warn them for Me (Ezekiel 33:7).

A Voice: She is a voice crying in the wilderness of life to many in this generation with the mandate to evangelize and prepare many for the coming of our Lord Jesus Christ...The voice of one crying in the wilderness, Prepare ye the way of the Lord, make his paths straight." (Matthew 3:3).

If you would like to invite Raeni Bankole as a teacher of the word at your seminar or church group program; please send an email to Nehemiahtroop@gmail.com.

Nehemiah Troop Prayer Ministry (NTPM)

...raising an army of intercessors

The Nehemiah Troop Prayer Ministry also known as "The Upper Room" is a weekly prayer school that has a mandate to raise fire-branded watchmen for the Kingdom of our Lord Jesus Christ. It follows after the vision of Nehemiah in the bible that didn't rest until he had rebuilt the walls of Jerusalem. He didn't do it alone; he had the king and his brethren(Nehemiah 2:1-20). Like Nehemiah, many of us today must be empowered like Joseph, Esther and Daniel to save our Father's house!

The vision of NTPM is to raise an army of intercessors all across the land and send out the clarion call for the prophet of nations to take their place on the prayer watches like Daniel who ushered their nation and generation into divine purpose.

There is a weekly phone conference every Saturday at 7:00 a.m. (CST) via freeconferencing.com: **Dial 530-881-1300 Access Code 328037**.

A live meeting also holds every 3rd Saturday of the month from 10 a.m. – 12 p.m. at the Schaumburg Renaissance Hotel.

For more details please view news and events at
www.empowermentmission.org or
the group page on facebook (Nehemiah Troop).

Nehemiah Troop Scholarship Fund (NTSF)

...empowering lives through education

Nehemiah Troop Scholarship Fund (NTSF) is a branch of the Raeni Bankole ministry that empowers young people in the Diaspora through education. The vision was born out of a need to help international students schooling abroad pay their tuition. As the coordinator, Raeni Bankole experienced first-hand what most international students with limited resources go through in order to stay in school. She came to the United States in 2001 to earn a masters degree but dropped out of the program after two semesters due to extreme financial hardship. It took over ten years to regain the dream of obtaining a masters' degree and the NTSF is a fulfillment of the vision to repair the breach and restore the path for many generations to dwell in.

The average cost of tuition per semester in the United States is $8000 - $10,000 and most international student cannot work outside the campus to support themselves. They usually have to drop out of school and defer the dream of furthering their education. It is extremely difficult to survive outside school because they also do not have employment authorization to make any living. Staying registered in school helps these young international students maintain F-1 status and achieve their academic dream. Please join us as we empower lives one day at a time through the Nehemiah Troop Scholarship Fund.

We want to hear from you!

Please send your comments about this book using the contact details below:

Phone: 630-936-8868
E-mail: nehemiahtroop@gmail.com
Website: www.empowermentmission.org

Please include your testimony of help received from this book when you write.
Your prayer requests are welcome.

You can order additional copies of this book or any other book by the author online @
www.amazon.com
or
simply send us an email or call us.

Dewalette Creations

Are you an author?

Would you like to have your book published?

It would be our delight to review your manuscript in preparation for an outstanding publication.

CONTACT US:

Phone:
(630) 481-6305

Email:
dewalette@gmail.com
info@dewalette.com